PARADISE LOST

NOTES

including

Complete Summary — Character Sketches

Selected Questions

Consulting Editor
James L. Roberts, Ph.D.
Department of English
University of Nebraska

Cliff's Notes
INCORPORATED

LINCOLN, NEBRASKA   68501

CONTENTS

PARADISE LOST

INTRODUCTION

THE mere suggestion of reading *Paradise Lost* may, for several reasons, strike terror into the modern heart. The book is full of allusions; the word order and involved sentences make understanding difficult; the work deals with what some consider an out-moded theology; and Milton wrote it almost three hundred years ago.

True, there are allusions, but one may enjoy much of *Paradise Lost* without understanding every reference. For the ambitious scholar an unabridged Webster's Dictionary, a Lempriere's Classical Dictionary, and a Bible will cover most of the allusions.

The word order and involved sentences will yield to patient reading, not word by word but thought by thought. One should remember also that the poem was dictated by Milton to his amanuensis, and undoubtedly read back and corrected. The lines should be heard as well as seen for full enjoyment.

In spite of the theology, the theme of the poem: life and death, is timeless, relevant to any time or place. Milton attempts to explain "Eternal Providence, and justify the ways of God to men."

If the reader feels that because this poem was written three hundred years ago, it must be out of date, he should apply a few of Milton's trenchant comments on affairs of the 17th century to conditions today. The nature of mankind has not changed much in three hundred years.

Milton, a blind old man, guided by an inner light, composed *Paradise Lost*. But he was much more than a lonely old poet. He had been an active participant in the life of England, first as a scholar and poet, then as public servant and statesman, and again as poet.

Born in 1608 in a cultivated and prosperous family, he developed a love of learning, of music and the arts. He knew well the Greek and Latin classics. Tending toward Puritanism in his strict moral outlook, his enthusiasm for temperance and chastity, and his disgust with what he considered the emptiness of the services of the Church of England, he was, on the other hand, a child of the Renaissance in his love for beauty and music and the wide experience of the classics. He foreshadowed the 18th Century romanticists in his love of nature and his belief that it was soothing to the spirit.

When he was about thirty years old, he took a trip abroad, was in Italy when he heard of impending civil war at home. He returned to England, lived in London and taught during the Civil War which began in 1642. About that time he began writing for the Puritan cause, particularly in favor of freedom of the press.

In 1642 he married a young girl of the Cavalier party, who soon deserted him and returned to her parents' home. Milton wanted a divorce which offended the Puritans. He had already opposed in his writings the Church of England.

His wife returned to him in 1645, died in 1652. In the meantime, King Charles was executed (1649), and when Cromwell became Lord Protector, Milton was invited to be Latin Secretary for the Council of State, a position something like a correspondent of foreign affairs.

At this time Milton's eyes began to fail, but he sacrificed his sight in service to the state, writing in defense of the execution of the king. Finally, completely blind, his wife dead, Milton continued as secretary under Cromwell until Cromwell's death and the end of the Protectorate.

With the Restoration, Milton was imprisoned (1660) for a time and some of his writings burned. He survived the great plague of 1665 which killed one-seventh of the population. The cessation of the plague coincided with the great London fire, in which Milton lost some property and possibly some manuscripts.

Although Milton had planned for years to do something epic, he actually began *Paradise Lost* about 1655. Even then his domestic life must have been difficult with orphaned daughters and a demanding mother-in-law. In 1656 he married Katherine Woodcock. She died within two years. In 1663 he married Elizabeth Minshull. *Paradise Lost* was published in 1674.

Although Milton's three daughters who lived with him in London, tried to help in his writing, they had little training, for it was the fashion then to think women incapable of learning. A recognized man of letters, Milton's admirers often visited him and helped by writing his dictation.

In *Paradise Lost* Milton utilizes all the broad resources of his study and his experience. Because of the breadth of both his learning and his life, the work stands as a rich comment on universal problems.

Because of the nature of the story, Milton allows many speakers, sometimes quoting other speakers. In order to help the reader find the material referred to in these notes, line numbers have been indicated.

In brief the book covers Satan's fall, the creation, man's fall, his provided redemption, and a preview of what would happen until the death of Christ, and the disintegration of the church up to the end of the world.

SUMMARIES AND COMMENTARIES

BOOK ONE

Summary

Milton invokes the Heavenly Muse, 1 ff., existent from the

beginning of time, to illumine him, raise his comprehension for this work, because Milton does not intend a middle flight over the mountain where the Greek Muses live, but something higher than has ever been attempted, that is, to justify God's ways to man.

First questioning the cause of sin, he begins the narrative, 34 ff. Satan's pride has cast him out of Heaven, hurled him into Hell where he and his crew lie vanquished, doomed though immortal, without hope in a place of "darkness visible" with "everburning Sulphur, unconsumed."

Satan notices, 78 ff., that Beelzebub, next in power and crime, welters by his side. Satan relates, 84 ff., how their situation has changed, how Hell contrasts with Heaven; but Satan does not repent. Although in despair, he vows "immortal hate and courage never to submit or yield." — war eternal.

Beelzebub admits, 128 ff., that God's physical force is superior, but thinks Satan's forces are invincible in mind and spirit. Beelzebub wonders if God means to leave them spirit and strength so they can suffer endlessly to satisfy his wrath, or so they can be God's slaves in Hell. What good is immortality if they have to endure eternal punishment?

Satan reacts at once, 157 ff., "Fallen Cherub, to be weak is miserable, Doing or Suffering..." He and his crew will find sole delight perverting God's plans into evil. In the meantime God has taken his warring angels back to Heaven; affairs have quieted, whether from scorn or satiate fury, Satan doesn't know. But he suggests they take advantage of the lull to get out of the lake of fire and reassemble troops on the dreary plain.

Satan is compared, 192 ff., to the mythical giants and to Leviathan. The Arch-fiend has been chained like a huge monster to the lake of fire. Milton tells the reader he would have stayed there unless God had let him up to prove his own damnation and the goodness of God. Satan rises from the lake; the flames roll off him; he flies to land — not land but solid rather than liquid fire.

Both Satan and Beelzebub think they have escaped not by God's sufferance but by their own power. Satan looks around and wonders, 242 ff., at what they have exchanged for Heaven. He repeats Beelzebub's thought that God reigns only in force not by reason—"he Whom Thunder hath made greater." The thesis of Satan's speech is:

"The mind is its own place, and in itself
Can make a Heaven of Hell, a Hell of Heaven.
.....
To reign is worth ambition, though in Hell:
Better to reign in Hell than serve in Heaven."

Satan suggests they get the rest of their friends out of the lake and see what can be done. Beelzebub says, 272 ff., that if the fallen angels hear Satan's voice, they'll revive.

Satan, 283 ff., goes to call his troops, scattered like leaves on the lake of fire. All Hell resounds at his call, 315 ff. He makes fun of them asking if this is their place of repose, if they are adoring their conqueror, waiting for him to nail them to the bottom of the lake with thunderbolts. The fallen angels hear and rise like the locusts in the plague of Egypt, and fill all the plain, more than the barbarians who will invade the Roman Empire.

These fallen angels now nameless in Heaven, have yet no names on earth where they will in time corrupt mankind. Beginning line 376 Milton asks the Muse for the earthly names of those who will be most active in polluting the worship of God. In rites for Moloch, the god of the Ammonites, children will be burned alive. Chemos, or Peor, god of lust will be worshipped in Moab. Baalim and Ashtaroth can choose any shape or sex. Israel will often forsake God for these bestial dieties, and therefore Israel will be defeated. To Astoreth or Astarte, the moon goddess of fertility and sexual love, Solomon will build a temple. Thammuz, lover of Astarte will cause Syrian damsels and Judah's daughters to lament in Pagan festival. Dagon's image will collapse before the Ark of God; Rimmon, god of Damascus, will corrupt Ahaz, king of Judah. Osiris, Isis, and Orus will be worshipped in the form of animals, like the

10

golden calf which Israel will make in Oreb. Belial, the most lewd, will have no temple but will turn priests, like Eli's sons, to atheism and will corrupt Sodom. Others will become Ionian and Greek gods.

The fallen angels revive with joy that their chief does not give up. Satan rises above despair and asks a Cherub to raise the imperial standard. Trumpets blow; all the legions cry out and frighten the reign of Chaos and Night. Ten thousand banners and a forest of spears stand in formation. Satan glows with pride and admiration. If all the future armies of earth were to be assembled, they would be as nothing compared to this host.

Here follows, 589 ff., a sympathetic picture of Satan. He weeps, feels responsible for their plight. Three times he tries to speak, three times chokes up. Finally he tells them, 622 ff., that no one could guess their defeat, since God's strength has never been tested. Now by guile and fraud, they will do what force hasn't done. "Who overcomes by force, hath overcome but half his foe." Satan relates the rumor of man's creation. This will be the first business of investiagion. He vows no peace, no submission.

His army flashes swords in defiance toward Heaven. Then Mammon, the least regarded in Heaven, leads a crew to dig gold to make a palace more wonderful than anything earth will ever have. Whereas earthly edifices take years for construction, this palace is built in an hour. Mulciber, the architect, had previously built in Heaven. The capitol of Hell is named Pandemonium. All the legions swarm into the palace which is so small that they change into dwarfs, and only the leaders remain gigantic.

Commentary

Milton opens his book with a prayer for help. Most of the action takes place in Hell with Satan the chief character. In the three descriptions of him the reader finds the first emphasizes his gigantic size and the horror of his fall; the second depicts his leadership; the third, the most sympathetic, shows that although lost, he retains much that is divine, which divinity makes him weep over those whom he has led into eternal Hell.

Clever, keen-minded Satan speaks like an orator. His words about the mind making its own Hell reflect Milton's philosophy of the supremacy of the mind. Milton repeats the same idea, IV, 20 ff., when describing Satan he says: "The Hell within him, for within him Hell."

Satan shows his sense of humor when he makes fun of the angels lying on the lake of fire by asking them if they are waiting to be nailed to the bottom. Humor shows in the name Pandemonium for Hell's capitol.

Book One establishes Satan as a powerful and sympathetic character. Man has been created. Satan plans to get revenge on God by seducing man, not by force but by guile. The plot and action of *Paradise Lost* evolve from these three facts. The conflict will be God versus Satan, Good versus Evil.

Much of the beauty of Milton's writing comes in his imaginative figures of speech: for example, he personifies the volcano Aetna, 233 ff., "Whose combustible And fueled entrails thence conceiving Fire." In line 351 ff., the earth pours men "from her frozen loins." Line 685 ff., says "Men... Rifled the bowels of their mother earth... Opened... a spacious wound, And digged out ribs of Gold."

Three similes to emphasize the number of fallen angels are: line 302, "Thick as Autumnal Leaves that strow the Brooks," line 340-341, "a pitchy cloud Of locusts" and line 351, a multitudinous army. In line 777 ff., the fallen angels changed to dwarfs are like the pygmies or elves of the forest.

BOOK TWO

Summary

Satan on his royal throne talks, 11 ff. As their leader through the law of Heaven and by their free choice, he will be first in danger. Since eminence brings danger, nobody can envy him his place and therefore, there will be unity in Hell. He asks advice as to what procedure is best: open war or deceit.

Moloch, the first speaker, prefers to be equal with God, but if he can't, he doesn't care what happens to him, so he has no fear. He advises open war, 51 ff., and in order to goad those who are still stunned from their fall, he reminds them that the proper motion of immortal spirits is upward. He asks what would be worse than eternal torture, certainly not complete destruction. And if they can't defeat Heaven, they can at least harass God and get revenge.

Belial, false and empty, talks, 118 ff., so that the worse appears the better. He would be for open war, since he lacks not hate; but Moloch bases his arguments on despair and dissolution with only possible revenge. Belial thinks they can't destroy Heaven; and if they end by letting Heaven destroy them, it will be a sad cure. "For who would lose, Though full of pain, this intellectual being?" Besides who knows if God could or would utterly destroy them? He would rather punish without end. Is Hell so bad? They first thought it a refuge from God. And if they anger God more, he could devise worse things for them, such as blowing up the flames or transfixing them on rocks or chaining them under the boiling sea.

Belial opposes war or guile, since God can see through these. Their doom is just; and he laughs at those who fight, lose, and then complain their fate. Maybe in time God will slacken the punishment; or maybe they'll get used to the odor and the flames. So Belial conceals his sloth as a desire for peace.

Mammon thinks, 229 ff., they have no chance in war; and even if God should offer them grace on terms of obedience, they would not be willing to kneel and sing hymns. He prefers "hard liberty before the easy yoke Of servile Pomp." Sometimes God chooses to dwell in darkness; so, they in Hell can imitate Heaven and use the gold and gems of Hell to make magnificence to rival Heaven. Like Belial, he thinks they'll get used to the climate. He opposes war.

The fallen angels applaud Mammon. When Beelzebub sees that they prefer peace and are afraid to fight God, he stands. Next to Satan in rank, he has not yet lost his princely bearing. He calls them offspring of Heaven, but suggests, 310 ff., they might be called the Princes of Hell. He reminds them that whether they dream of war or peace, God will have his way and rule them anyhow. They have lost the war; no peace terms have been offered. They want no peace, only hate and revenge. There is another world, where a new race has been created, like to the angels but a little lower in form. This new creature has God's favor. Beelzebub thinks they should investigate and perhaps drive out the new creatures with hell fire, or seduce them and cause God to hate and destroy them, a sweet revenge. Isn't this a better plan than to sit "in darkness here Hatching vain Empires?"

In fact Beelzebub is speaking Satan's plan. The crowd likes this suggestion of revenge. Beelzebub commends their judgment, 390 ff., and says if they can take over this nearer place, they may get to bask in the light of Heaven, and possibly re-enter Heaven from this closer area. But who is to go find out about the new creation?

Fear immobilizes them, but Satan, still their monarch, offers to investigate, 430 ff. First he reviews the dangers: the prison of Hell out of which he must break, the unformed Night through which he must travel, and other unknown dangers. Willing to go, he would be unfit to rule if danger kept him back. The higher the position, the greater hazard he should be willing to bear. He advises them in his absence to make Hell as comfortable as possible and keep a strict watch for danger. He forbids anyone to go with him, rises and closes the council before any one can offer to go with him; for although the offer would be refused, the one so offering would thereby gain prestige. But the fallen angels are more afraid of Satan's voice than of the dark journey. They rise and praise him; for spirits damned do not lose all their virtue.

After the council ends, a trumpet salutes Satan; and the crowd disperses to do whatever each may like until Satan returns. They run races, promote contests like those of the Olympian games held in honor of Zeus or the Pythian held in honor of Apollo, athletic festivals of ancient Greece. Here follow classical references to various feats of the gods, such as Alcides (Hercules), when poisoned by a robe his wife has given him, throws the messenger who has brought the robe, into the sea and burns himself to death in Mt. OEta.

Those indifferent to athletics sing so beautifully that the harmony suspends Hell. Others meditate on fixed fate, free will, foreknowledge, wandering in mental mazes without end. Others explore Hell, finding four rivers: the Styx, river of hate; Acheron, river of sorrow; Cocytus, river of wailing; and Phlegethon, river of burning. Lethe, the river of forgetting, is not one of the four, and no one may drink of it, for then he would forget everything. Beyond the fiery Hell, lies a frozen Hell, so that victims may be burned then frozen. Harpies chase the damned from the flame to the ice. Medusa stands to prevent a sip of the water of Lethe. The searchers find only horrors throughout Hell.

Meanwhile Satan flies up to the nine gates of Hell, 629 ff., and finds a creature half woman and half snake. Around her are hell-hounds barking; but at any disturbance, they creep inside her and bark and howl. With the woman is another shape black as night, fierce as fury, terrible as Hell. He carries a dart and wears a crown. Satan does not fear him, but asks, 681 ff., why he bars the gates and says he means to pass.

Then the goblin asks, 689 ff., if he is that traitor angel. The goblin says he rules there, and he will send Satan back to his punishment. The shapeless horror grows and threatens; but Satan unafraid, burns like a comet. They are about to attack each other, when the snaky sorceress, Sin, reveals that Satan is her father and the monster, Death, their incestuous son. Revolted, Satan does not recognize her at first, 737 ff., but she reminds him, 747 ff., of how she came out of the left side of his head, a glorious shape, named Sin. Then she and Satan conceived Death; but after he was born, her body turned half snake. Then Death bred in her the hell-hounds which return into her body and gnaw at her bowels. Death would like to devour his mother, Sin; but he knows that if she dies, he also dies.

Then Satan with soft words, 817 ff., explains that he has come to set them all free, that he goes to seek the place where a new creature has been created, that he will return and take Sin and Death with him to enjoy the new land.

Sin says, 850 ff., that she is supposed to keep the gates shut; but she doesn't care for God's commands. She will obey Satan. She opens the gates of Hell; but she cannot shut them. The flames illumine chaos. Satan flies into the abyss, is caught in a vacuum and drops ten thousand fathoms; but some cloud hurls him up again. He flounders half on foot, half flying. Finally he hears noises and sees the throne of Chaos and his pavillion.

Satan tells Chaos, 968 ff., that he hasn't come to spy, but explains his errand and suggests that the new world might be so contaminated that it could be turned back into chaos. Naturally Chaos likes this idea. He recognizes Satan, 990 ff., says he saw the war and the expulsion from Heaven. He complains that Hell and Earth have both been cut out of his domain; but if Satan can spread havoc, spoil, and ruin, he will be glad. He speeds Satan on his way, saying it isn't too far yet. Satan takes off, having a difficult time to make earth. At last he draws near enough to see the battlements of Heaven, and the new-made earth, hanging by a golden chain.

Commentary

The action begins in Hell, and ends where Satan sights the new-made earth. New characters introduced are Sin, Death and Chaos. Principal speakers in the council on what to do, have been mentioned before. Each speaker reveals his own nature. Moloch is for action, Belial is for ease. Mammon wants to get his hands into the gold; and Beelzebub wants to spread evil. Satan reveals his psychological understanding when he tells Sin and Death he is working for them, and then tells Chaos the same thing—so they will cooperate with him. Chaos, disorganized in every respect, is eager to have Satan ruin what he can.

As in Book One, Milton lets the demons declare some moral truths—truths dear to Milton: 432-433

> "........long is the way
> And hard, that out of Hell leads up to light..."

and 497-498

"........men only disagree
Of Creatures rational..."

There are evidences of Milton's experience with civil war and popular leaders. Perhaps he had known men who would argue the viewpoints which he gives to leading demons. Milton had sat in meetings of English leaders where the rational creatures disagreed. Milton makes fun of the Presbyterians with his lines about the demons pondering, 559-561,

"Of Providence, Foreknowledge, Will, and Fate,
Fixed Fate, free will, foreknowledge absolute,
And found no end, in wandering mazes lost."

One of Milton's favorite word uses appears several times in this book: that is the use of an adjective for a noun, as line 278, "The sensible of pain;" line 406, "the palpable obscure;" line 409, "the vast abrupt;" line 980, "I travel this profound." Another characteristic of Milton is the use of opposites as in line 594-595, "the parching Air Burns frore [frozen]," or line 623, "Created evil, for evil only good."

The classic references abound. In the first few lines he compares Satan's throne to all the most splendid wealth of India, Persia, and the Orient. Tartarean sulphur, line 69, means infernal sulphur; and Atlantean shoulders, line 306, refer to Atlas who bore the world on his shoulders. The Serbonian bog, line 592, refers to Lake Serbonis in Lower Egypt. Damiata is a city at the mouth of the Nile.

The harpies and the Medusa are natural inhabitants of Hell, living there when the fallen angels arrive. Medusa, whose hair was made of snakes, turns anyone who sees her to stone. Tantalus, whose punishment is to stand in water, perishes eternally of thirst for he may not drink. Hydras are nine-headed serpents; and Chimaera is a fire-breathing monster. Scylla, a beautiful nymph made hideous by Circe, threw herself into the sea. The night-hag, line 662, is Hecate who drinks the blood of babies.

In line 709 Satan is compared to Ophiuchus in the arctic sky. This constellation is not in the northern heavens; but Satan was supposed to have come from the north, therefore the confusion. Bellona was the Roman goddess of war, line 922. Syrtix, 939, means quicksand.

Usually Milton's classical and other allusions occur when he wishes to make a simile. In talking of Satan's journey to earth, he compares it to Argo's passage through Bosporus, (which refers to Jason's search for the Golden Fleece) or to Ulysses shunning Charybdis, (which refers to the adventures of Ulysses in the *Odyssey*).

Milton's choice of words that sound like the thing named (onomatopoeia) appears line 880 ff.,

> "With impetuous recoil and jarring sound
> The infernal doors, and on their hinges grate
> Harsh Thunder, that the lowest bottom shook
> Of Erebus." (Hell).

A similar use of words where the sense is heightened by repetition comes in line 185, "Unrespited, unpitied, unreprieved," and lines 621-622,

> "Rocks, Caves, Lakes, Fens, Bogs, Dens, and shades
>   of death,
>   A Universe of death..."

Love of music appears in line 552 ff.,

> "Their song was partial, but the harmony
>   ....
>   Suspended Hell."

BOOK THREE

Summary
Like Book One this book starts with a prayer, a hymn to light.
Milton says, 23 ff., that light

> "Revisit'st not these eyes, that roll in vain
> To find thy piercing ray, and find no dawn."

> "............Thus with the Year
> Seasons return; but not to me returns
> Day, or the sweet approach of Even or Morn,
> Or sight of vernal bloom, or Summer's Rose,
> Or flocks, or herds, or human face divine;"

He wishes that he might be equal in fame as he is in fate with various of the famous blind persons of mythology. He implores inward light, 51ff., that he may see things invisible to mortal sight.

He begins the story, 56 ff., of how God sits with his Son and watches Adam and Eve in the garden, how he sees Satan winging his way up from Hell to Earth. God asks his Son, 80 ff., if he sees the anger and revenge of Satan ready to seduce man. God says man will fall through his own choice; for he is made either to stand or fall. Free will is inherent in all God's creation. If men weren't free, they could not give proof of fidelity. They could do only what they had to do, and this is not worship. God makes a point of the difference between Satan and man: Satan and his angels fell by self-deception. Man will fall because of Satan's temptation, and therefore may be redeemed.

All Heaven rejoices to hear God's word, and the Son speaks, 144 ff. Mercy is sweet. He rejoices that man will be forgiven. If man were doomed to Hell, Satan's revenge would be complete. Or, if man were destroyed, that would only please Satan and defeat God.

God commends the Son, 168 ff., "Man shall not quite be lost, but saved who will." God will put a conscience in man; and if man will listen, he will be led from light to light, and arrive safely. Only those who do not choose God will be excluded from his grace. But this is not all. Either man or justice must die to satisfy the law of Heaven. Or someone must die for man. Silence follows. Nobody offers to die for man. Then the Son says, 227 ff., he will pay the price and forfeit all that Death can take. He knows God will not leave him in the grave, but will raise him victorious, and deprive Death of his power, and bring the redeemed children of Earth home to Heaven and eternal joy.

All Heaven glows with admiration. God speaks of his love for his Son, 274 ff., and his love for mankind, which love will let him lose his Son for a while to save a whole race. The Son will take Adam's place, but he shall lose nothing by his sacrifice. He is God's Son more by merit than by birthright. God says the Son shall reign eternal, the Son of God and man. The Son shall judge all men, sentence the evil men and angels to Hell, seal it shut, and burn the world. From its ashes will come a new Heaven and Earth for the just. Then the regal scepter will no more be needed because "God shall be All in All." He calls the angels to adore the Son who has made this possible.

Heaven rings with jubilee. The angels make wreaths of amarant, a flower that does not wither, then take their harps and sing. Beginning 372 ff., Milton uses direct address to God and the Son, telling of how the angels praise the Father, whom no one can see, how creatures see the Father in the Son. The angels sing of the fight with rebellious angels and how the Son chased them out, and how mercy will be shown to mankind because of the Son.

While the angels are singing, 416 ff., Satan alights on the "windy Sea of Land" which will in time be the place where all vain things go, a Vale of Vanity. Like a vulture, Satan seeks his prey. Some will in time dream that vain persons and things go to the Moon; but Milton says translated saints or middle spirits will live there. But in the Vale of Vanity will live the men who built the Tower of Babel, Empedocles who will wish to be thought a god and so will jump into a volcano, or Cleombrotus who will jump into the sea after reading Plato on the immortality of the soul. Also in this Vale will be embryos, idiots, pilgrims who will look in the wrong places for the Son of God, and priests and monks. All the trumperies of the church and the priests will, when they go up to St. Peter, be blown back to this Paradise of Fools.

Satan now sees some light, sees the stairway to Heaven, which is let down over the Jasper Sea to take people into Heaven. The stairway not always visible is let down for Satan to see; and just under it, he sees a passage down to Earth—a wide passage which will narrow in later years.

Satan full of wonder and envy observes the world. He flies down through the stars that dot the Earth's sky, heads toward the sun, alights there in a region of radiant light. Milton here wonders about the beauty of the sun and its virtue, 606 ff., how it can produce such marvelous air, water, and beauty on the earth.

Satan then notices an angel keeping watch on the sun, and decides to inquire the way to Paradise. But first he changes himself into a "stripling Cherub" and appears as a lesser angel of light. The Archangel Uriel does not recognize him. Satan asks, 654 ff., where man dwells. He praises God and his wisdom in casting out the rebels, and Uriel does not perceive Satan for what he is, 682 ff.,

> "For neither Man or Angel can discern
>   Hypocrisy, the only evil that walks
>   Invisible, except to God alone."

So Uriel commends the Cherub's interest in God's creation, 694 ff., tells of how he saw the world created, and darkness flee, the elements separated and the stars put in place. He shows which orb is Earth, how it is lighted by the sun and moon. He points out Paradise where Adam lives. Satan bows low, flies down to earth, and alights on Niphates' top.

Commentary

When Milton refers to his blindness at the beginning of this section, the reader should remember that not only does *Paradise Lost* tell about God's way to man, but also reflects Milton's attempt to explain his personal tragedies and those of England.

His remarks about the Vale of Vanity and the Paradise of Fools give him a chance to comment on the Church, 489 ff.,

> "..........then might ye see
> Cowls, Hoods and Habits with their wearers tossed
> And fluttered into Rags; then Reliques, Beads,
> Indulgences, Dispenses, Pardons, Bulls,
> The sport of Winds: All these upwhirled aloft
> Fly o'er the backside of the World far off..."

His expression "backside of the World" indicates his opinion of the current church practices. He scoffs at Presbyterian predestination, with God's speech that worship without free will is not worship at all.

Action in Book Three begins with God and the Son and the angels in Heaven, where a scene parallel to one in Book Two is enacted. In Book Two Satan asks who will go find man, the victim for seduction and revenge. No one offers; so Satan says he will go. In Book Three God asks who will die for man. No one offers; then the Son says he will die. The two are set up as opposites with man the source of conflict.

After Satan has rested on the sun, he flies down and alights on Earth. The fall of man is foreseen, the redemption promised.

Milton's use of repetition of short words for an effect of cluttered monotony may be seen in the above quotation in regard to the trivia of the church. Another example of a quotation using contrast and repetition is, 298 ff.,

"So Heavenly love shall outdo Hellish hate,
Giving to death, and dying to redeem,
So dearly to redeem what Hellish hate
So easily destroyed...."

Two more examples of art by contrast are, 380 ff.,

"Dark with excessive bright" and, 686 ff.,

"And oft though wisdom wake, suspicion sleeps
At wisdom's Gate, and to simplicity
Resigns her charge, while goodness thinks no ill
Where no ill seems."

BOOK FOUR

Summary
    Satan now nears the Garden of Eden. Milton wishes, 1ff., that someone would cry loud enough to warn man against his coming. But Satan is not entirely happy in his own mind, 18 ff.,

"......... horror and doubt distract
His troubled thoughts, and from the bottom stir
The Hell within him, for within him Hell
He brings, and round about him, nor from Hell
One step no more than from himself can fly
By change of place."

    Satan's conscience, not yet dead, troubles him. First he calls to the Sun, 32 ff., not with love but with hate because the Sun's beams remind him of Heaven, of his sin. Satan admits that God did not deserve what Satan did, that his sin is pride because he wanted to be the highest without paying gratitude, not understanding "that a grateful mind by owing, owes not."

    For a minute Satan thinks that if he hadn't held such a high place in Heaven, he might not have fallen, but then he realizes that some other Power might have done just what he did, and he, Satan, would have been drawn away. He has to admit that he had free will, that some angels had remained faithful, and that he has chosen the worst. And again he repeats, "Which way I fly is Hell: myself am Hell."

Even as pride was his fall, so pride keeps him from submission which he knows is the only answer. But the fallen angels adore him though he knows that he is supreme only in misery. And if God would take him back, how does Satan know that he might not again yield to desire for a higher place and so fall again and to a worse state. So, he turns his thought to man and concludes his meditation with, 108 ff.,

> "So farewell Hope, and with Hope farewell Fear,
> Farewell Remorse: All Good to me is lost;
> Evil, be thou my Good; by thee at least
> Divided Empire with Heaven's King I hold
> By thee, and more than half perhaps will reign;
> As Man ere long, and this new World shall know."

Satan decides for evil and with this thought his face which he had disguised to fool Uriel, undergoes a change from anger to envy and despair. Then Satan realizes that his face will betray him, and he attempts to restore his cherubic countenance, "the first That practiced falsehood under saintly show." But Uriel has seen his disfiguration and knows he is the evil spirit of whom he has been warned.

Satan goes on toward Paradise; and the reader glimpses Eden, surrounded by a thicket and screened by trees. Within the wall of trees are fruit trees with blossoms and fruits of rainbow colors. Satan breathes the pure air which could dispel all sadness except despair, Satan's permanent mental condition.

Satan plans to enter Eden; but the undergrowth is too thick. The only gate lies on the east side. This Satan disdains, jumps over the trees and alights in the Tree of Life, like a cormorant, not benefitting from the Tree of Life, but planning the death of Mankind. Here Milton moralizes, 201 ff.,

> ".....So little knows
> Any but God alone, to value right
> The good before him, but perverts best things
> To worst abuse, or to their meanest use."

Now Milton describes Paradise, the Tree of Life, the Tree of Knowledge, the river that flows through Eden, the flowers and beauties. Milton mentions that spring lives universal, and says that Eden surpasses any paradise mentioned in the classics.

Man is noble, tall, and "God-like erect." Woman worships the God that is in Man. The pair, innocent, pure and without shame, sit down to a supper of fruits while the animals play around them. The sun sets and the stars come out.

Speechless at first, Satan sinks into sadness and at last talks to himself, 358 ff. Man, he sees, is little lower than the angels, and he could love him so easily for he is so like God. Yet, Satan does not change his desire to make man one with himself. Again ambition drives him on, although he pities man's fate. Shortly before, he blamed himself for his situation, now he blames God for the fall. Himself damned, he must take everyone possible with him. Thus he excuses himself and alights among the animals to change himself into their kind so he may spy on Adam and Eve. Milton compares him to a tiger, stalking two fawns.

Adam extols the goodness of God, 411ff., and says it is not a hard thing to be forbidden the Tree of Knowledge, the sole test of obedience. They must praise God and care for the garden he has given them.

Eve answers, 440 ff., that she is doubly blest because she has both Adam and God, where Adam has no one his equal. She remembers her first moments of life, beside a river, her admiration for her own image, and the voice promising motherhood of the human race, which led her to Adam. When she saw Adam she preferred her own image in the lake until Adam called her to him.

After their talk they embrace; and Satan full of envy can

scarcely bear to look at them, but turns aside and plans their doom. He remarks, 505 ff., that one of Hell's torments is desire. He remembers that the Tree of Knowledge is forbidden and asks himself if they live only because of ignorance. He will excite their minds with desire to know, get them to taste and die. Meanwhile he will look around for some heavenly spirit which can give him information to help destroy the pair.

As the sun sets, and while Gabriel guards the eastern gate of Eden, watching the angels exercise in heroic games, Uriel comes to warn Gabriel that an evil spirit has passed. Gabriel has seen no one, but he admits the difficulty, 577 ff., of keeping out spiritual substance with corporeal bars. But if any evil one is in the garden, Gabriel will find him before morning.

Now the sun has set and Adam and Eve are about to retire. Adam says they need rest for tomorrow's work. He praises work as showing the care of God, tells what they will do on the morrow.

Eve agrees, 635 ff.,

"God is thy Law, thou mine; to know no more
Is woman's happiest knowledge and her praise."

Paradise would not be sweet without Adam. She wonders who enjoys the beauty while they sleep.

Adam answers, 660 ff., that the stars have their circuit to make; for if they didn't shine, total Darkness might regain possession. Even if there were no men, God would not lack praise nor heaven spectators. "Millions of spiritual Creatures walk the Earth Unseen." Adam and Eve have heard celestial voices.

Adam and Eve pause to worship before they enter their special bower, framed in laurel and myrtle. They thank God, 724 ff., for promising children. Here Milton intrudes to extol the virtues of true marriage.

About nine o'clock the Cherubim go out for the nightwatch.

Gabriel sends Uzziel and half the angels south, the others north, 782 ff.; they are to meet in the west. He calls Ithuriel and Zephon to search the garden for an evil spirit.

They find Satan in the form of a toad, whispering discontented thoughts and vain desires in Eve's ear. When an angel touches him, he returns to his own grisly form which startles the angels. They ask him, 823 ff., who he is. Satan answers that if they don't know him, they must be pretty low class because all important angels know him.

Zephron says, 835 ff., that he has changed from what he was in Heaven, that he must come and account for himself. Satan feels "how awful goodness is" and regrets his "luster visibly impaired" but says he will fight only the best, not lesser angels. Gabriel comes near, identifies Satan, 866 ff., asks him what he has done. Satan says Gabriel isn't very bright or he would know that anyone would try to better his plight. God will have to put stronger bars on Hell to hold him. The fact they found him at Eve's ear doesn't prove a thing.

Gabriel taunts Satan's wisdom, 904 ff., which consists of flying from pain, and asks why Satan came alone, weren't the others suffering?

Satan protests his bravery, 925 ff., but claims he came first as a faithful leader to see if they ought to settle on Earth. Gabriel accuses Satan of double talk in first saying he flew from pain, then in saying he came to spy. He questions Satan's use of the word faithful. Gabriel commands him to go back to Hell or be dragged in chains.

Satan calls Gabriel a "Proud limitary Cherub," 971 ff., and says when he is Gabriel's captive, they may talk of chains. Meanwhile the host of good angels gathers thick as heads of wheat ready for harvest. Satan puffs himself up until he reaches the sky, with Horror sitting on his crest. There might have been a terrible battle, but God hung forth his golden scales with two weights showing the consequence of parting and of fighting. Gabriel admits they both fight with borrowed powers and nothing but what God wills can happen. Since Satan's fate is defeat, he turns and flees taking with him the shades of night.

Commentary

Physical action takes place in the Garden of Eden. Psychological action begins with Satan honestly admitting that his fall is his own fault, that God is justified. The reader sees his choice of evil, his physical deterioration, his toad-like disguise, his loss of glory, his expansion to fill earth and sky with horror.

The reader sees Adam and Eve in their innocence, under the curse of Satan's eyes. Knowledge of what will happen to them makes their happiness poignant. Man is God-like erect. Eve, with a show of feminine vanity prefers her own image in the water. Milton believes women inferior to men; but that was a common conviction of his day. He does not believe in celibacy, praises marriage, deplores court amours.

Although Milton advocates free will throughout, he admits at the end of this section, that Satan's fate is to lose — which would almost sound like predestination.

Milton uses Satan's outer appearance as a gauge to measure his inner state. His luster is visibly impaired. The fact that Satan mourns not his inner loss but his outward appearance evidences his pride. Milton insists that one carries his own inward Hell and he can not escape it.

Psychologically Milton plants the idea for Eve's sin when Adam says they must not think hard of God for denying them the Tree of Knowledge.

Milton's humor, probably gained from sitting in sessions of government committees, shows in Satan's scornful repartee with various angels and their cutting replies.

Milton describes landscapes, seascapes, sunrises, and sunsets. As compensation for blindness he recalls all the beauties he has seen with those read about and those imagined.

BOOK FIVE

Summary
   Morning comes. Adam awakens, wonders that Eve still sleeps
in a disturbed condition. He calls her to come and see how their
plants are growing. She embraces Adam and relates a dream of a
voice calling her, 28 ff., saying beauty is vain if no one sees it. At
first she thought it was Adam and went to find him, but at last she
found herself by the Tree of Knowledge of Good and Evil. A being
whom she thought an angel, talked to the tree, tasted the fruit. Although Eve was horrified, the being experienced no evil, only enjoyment of the fruit. He asked Eve to taste so she might be a goddess
and fly with him. He held some to her mouth. It smelled so good she
tasted, then flew into the clouds and watched the beautiful world be-
low. Suddenly her guide left; she sank into sleep. She is relieved to
find it but a dream.

   Her dream disturbs Adam, 95 ff., and he cannot understand
where evil can have originated. He thinks false Fancy has put odd
bits together, producing weird shapes. He thinks her dream the re-
sult of their talk the previous evening; but there are strange addi-
tions. He reassures her, tells her evil can come into a mind and if
unapproved, go and leave not a trace. He hopes that what in sleep
she abhorred, she would not consent to do while awake. Then cheer-
ful, he suggests they go out to see the flowers.

   Eve cries, but he kisses her and they go out just as the sun rises.
They pray, 153 ff., saying God's goodness shows in his works. They
ask all beings to praise God: the Angels, the Morning Star, the Sun
and the Moon, and other wandering Fires that move, the Elements,
the Mists and Exhalations, the Winds, the Pines, Fountains, Birds,
and all living things. Adam asks God to dispel any evil of the night,
as day dispels the night.

   Then with peaceful thoughts they go to cut back boughs and
train vines. God sees them and calls Raphael, 224 ff., to warn them

against Satan who designs against the whole human race. Raphael will have half a day to make clear to Adam and Eve that they have free will, free but mutable. They will meet guile, not violence.

Raphael flies through Heaven's gate, toward Earth, looking like a phoenix; but when he comes to the eastern cliff of Paradise, he alights and returns to his proper shape with six wings. All the angel bands rise to salute him. He goes through perfumed fields, through the spicy forest. Adam sitting in the door of his cool bower during the hot noon hour, sees him coming. He tells Eve, 308 ff., who is preparing lunch, that they have a guest and she must prepare the best.

Eve says, 321 ff., that with such abundance, there is no need to store things, unless storage improves them. She will get the greatest delicacies. Her mind intend on a well balanced meal, she makes drinks of berries, cream of kernels. After placing the food in dishes, Eve spreads roses and sweet shrubs on the ground.

Meantime Adam, dignified but not pompous, humble but not fawning, goes out to meet the guest. Adam addresses the guest as a Native of Heaven, 361 ff., and invites him to rest and eat until the heat is past.

The Angel says, 372 ff., that is why he came, and that Adam is so created and his home so arranged that heavenly guests may visit. He will stay until evening. They go into the lodge where Eve waits to entertain her heavenly guest. He greets her, 388 ff., "Hail, Mother of Mankind," and says her children will be more numerous than all the fruits heaped on the table.

Adam invites the angel to eat, 397 ff.; although he isn't sure that celestial natures can eat earthly food, he knows it all comes from the same God.

The angel explains, 404 ff., that man is part spiritual and whatever man has, can also be used by celestial persons, that the "grosser feeds the purer." He explains by saying that earth feeds the sea, both feed the air, and the air feeds fires ethereal. The angel eats with real hunger, contrary, says Milton, to the theologians who deny substance to angels. Milton also interposes a comment on Eve and her innocent nakedness, because this was before any "injured Lover's Hell."

Adam asks the angel to compare heavenly fruits with earthly, 461 ff. The angel says, 469 ff., that all things come from one first source. He enlarges the theme of the lower feeding the higher. If man be obedient, he too may grow until his body turns at last all to spirit. Meanwhile, he advises Adam to be happy where he is.

Adam questions the angel, 507 ff., about the phrase, "if Ye be found Obedient." The angel repeats the message, 519 ff., that man is free, but not immutable. He can err. It depends on man's free will because 532 ff.,

> "Can hearts not free, be tried whether they serve
> Willing or no, who will but what they must
> By Destiny, and can no other choose?"

Some have chosen disobedience and have fallen into Hell.

Adam wants only to serve the Maker, 544 ff.; but he has curiosity about the rebellion in Heaven; and since the afternoon lies before them, he would like to hear more.

Raphael says, 563 ff., he will try to explain by comparing celestial things with earthly. He tells how Chaos reigned before there was a world. One day God called all the orders and told them, 600 ff., that his only begotten Son would be chief of Heaven. Everyone seemed pleased, but Lucifer was not. That evening on pretext of preparing to entertain God and the Son, Lucifer drew all his hosts off to the North to prepare treason.

Aware of this God told the Son, 719 ff., that rebellion was coming, that the forces should gather. The Son answered, 735 ff., that he was ready to try himself in battle.

Meanwhile Satan had taken his leagues to the North, gathered them round him and said, 772 ff., that another had usurped their power. He called their worship of God and his Son, "prostration vile." It was bad enough to pay tribute to God, but now their duty was to be doubled; therefore they should cast off the yoke. They were equals with God and should govern, not serve.

Only one angel, Abdiel, argued this proposition, 809 ff. He called Satan blasphemous, false, and proud. He said that God made them and his purpose would be to make them more, not less. The appointment of the Son was for benefit, not degradation. The Son had helped in the creation of the very angels who were rebelling.

Satan said, 853 ff., that he hadn't heard that before. He asked Abdiel if he remembered being made and how he came to know so much. So far as Satan knew, they were self-begot, self-raised, full of their own power; and they should try by proof to see who were strongest. He told Abdiel to go tell God and to hurry before he got hurt. All the angels applauded, but Abdiel paid no attention and declared, 877 ff., that Satan was doomed. Abdiel flew away amid their scorn, not because he was afraid but because any minute God might send devouring flames to destroy them.

Faithful Abdiel turned back toward God, leaving Satan and his angels doomed to destruction.

Commentary

In order to get in backflashes on the war in heaven, Milton has the angel relate the story to Adam and Eve. The action, then, starts in the Garden of Eden, flashes back to Heaven before the fall. Little progress is made here in character development. The book consists mostly of narrative.

In the previous book Eve has asked Adam; who enjoys the stars and the night while we are asleep? Now Satan uses the same idea to snare Eve. In her dream he says that beauty is vain if none regard, 43-44. Likewise Milton foreshadows Eve's fall by the content of the evil dream.

Certain Miltonian themes are again expressed, 235 ff.,

> "Happiness in his power left free to will,
> Left to his own free Will, his Will though free
> Yet mutable."

He scoffs at theologians who think angels do not have real substance by telling how the angel ate. He repeats his belief in free will by saying that hearts not free can not be said to serve, and his emphasis on the dignity of man by the fact that he may entertain angels.

When Abdiel stands alone in spite of scorn, the reader must remember that Milton stood alone various times during his career in political and religious England. He speaks for himself as well as Abdiel.

Light has a special fascination for Milton; it symbolizes all good. Two descriptions of sunrise are; 1 ff.,

> "Now Morn her rosy steps in the Eastern Clime
> Advancing, sowed the Earth with Orient Pearl..."

and, 139 ff.,

> "...and the Sun, who scarce up risen
> With wheels yet hovering o'er the Ocean brim,
> Shot parallel to the earth his dewy ray,
> Discovering in wide Landscape all the east
> Of Paradise...."

Two metaphors that illustrate Milton's rich speech, 215 ff.,

> "....or they led the vine
> To wed her elm; she spoused about him twines
> Her marriageable arms, and with her brings
> Her dower, the adopted clusters, to adorn
> His barren leaves."

and, 394 ff.,

> "....though Spring and Autumn here
> Danced hand in hand."

BOOK SIX

Summary

Raphael continues his story. Abdiel, unpursued, flew back to Heaven and found all the armies of Heaven ready to fight. God, in a golden cloud, commended him, 29 ff., saying how difficult it is to bear universal reproach, more difficult than to endure violence. God commissioned Michael and Gabriel to drive the evil ones from God and bliss into the gulf of Tartarus (Hell).

Then clouds began to darken and the trumpet blew. Satan and his hordes appeared in the North; and the battle began, both sides fighting bravely. Abdiel wanted to reprimand Satan once more, 114 ff.,

> "Oh, Heaven! that such resemblance of the Highest
> Should yet remain, where faith and realty
> Remain not..."

Abdiel would try in arms what he knew to be weak in reason. He taunted Satan with wanting God's throne. He asked if there weren't a few more of Satan's group who preferred faith, although he, Abdiel alone, had left the rebellious armies, 142 ff.,

> "...but thou seest
> All are not of thy train; there be who Faith
> Prefer, and Piety to God,...now learn too late
> How few sometimes may know, when thousands err."

Satan said, 156 ff., that Abdiel had opposed a third part of the gods; Satan had thought liberty and Heaven were one; but some preferred through laziness to serve, eat and sing, rather than be free. He accused Abdiel of wanting to be with the minstrels of Heaven.

Abdiel answered, 172 ff., that servitude is to serve the unwise or him who has rebelled against his worthier. He told Satan to go ahead and reign in Hell, but to expect chains. For greeting Abdiel hit Satan such a blow that the Devil was thrown back ten paces, like a mountain pushed out of its way ahd half sunk with its pines. The rebels were astonished and enraged. The good angels rejoiced; and then Michael ordered the trumpet blown; and the war began, each one fighting as if the whole victory depended on him.

All day the battle raged until Michael and Satan met in personal combat. Michael wanted to finish the "Intestine War" right then. He reproved Satan, 262 ff., for beginning misery where none was, and said he would be cast into Hell. Satan said, 282 ff., not to talk so big, for none of the rebellious angels had run. They were going to dwell free right there, if not to rule. Satan would not retreat. They rushed into conflict like two planets crashing in mid-air.

Michael's sword was stronger, and it cut Satan's in half and wounded Satan, who then first knew pain. But his substance, being of different material from mortals, closed and healed itself. Satan's angels took him back and laid him in his chariot. He was full of shame, of humbled pride.

Meanwhile Gabriel fought Moloch. Their own innocence helped the good angels. Night drew on, and a temporary truce was called. Satan talked to his crew, 418 ff. If they had stood one day, they could stay eternally. Heaven's most powerful had not subdued them. They had not been so well armed as they should. They must get something better.

Nisroch said, 451 ff., they could live without pleasure but not in pain; so whatever would most quickly win the war, they should obtain. Satan said, 470 ff., what they needed wasn't yet invented, but there were materials underground that would help. He suggested metal guns, full of dark thunder. They could build these before dawn.

Satan's words cheered them. At this point the angel Raphael warns Adam, 501 ff., that on earth men might get the same idea about guns. Meanwhile Satan's armies dug the metal and built the guns. When morning came, the good angels stood ready. They thought Satan had fled, but soon he came. Zophiel urged the angels,

537 ff., to prepare for something strange.

Satan's group came in tight formation, made a square which hid the guns, and said, 558 ff., that they came seeking peace and composure and were ready with open breast to receive the Heavenly angels. So Satan scoffed, while the rebels fell back and revealed the guns, which belched chained thunderbolts, causing the good angels, burdened in armor, to go rolling. Satan thought this amusing. He called them to come, 609 ff.; he was ready to make peace; and maybe he should state his proposals again.

Then Belial said, 621 ff., they had sent terms of weight, but the good angels hadn't understood correctly, meaning they had fallen. So the evil ones made fun of the good ones and had no doubt of victory. For a little while the good hosts were troubled; then enraged they threw away their arms and tore up the mountains with all their pines and stones and used them as weapons. When the evil hosts saw the mountains about to be thrown on them, they feared being crushed in their armor. They took hills and fought so that the battle seemed underground.

All Heaven was being torn apart. God called his Son, 680 ff., and said that two days had passed, and that since the disobedient were formed equal in creation to the obedient, their power was too well balanced, since God had suspended the doom that sin of itself brings. So the war found no conclusion. The third day the Son was to finish the war, so that all the Universe might know him to be Heir and Mightiest.

The Son spoke, 723 ff., that he would do what God asked. He could represent either God's love or his terror. He took the Chariot of Paternal Deity, drove forth. The obedient armies joined him. He sent back the uprooted hills, restored order. Satan and his army saw this; but out of despair they gained hope. They grieved to see the Son's glory, determined to win against him or fall in universal ruin.

The Son asked the saints to rest, 801 ff. To him was reserved the punishment for this crew. They had despised and envied the

Son, and God had appointed him to seal their doom. Then he changed his countenance into terror and drove on toward the armies of Satan. When he rose over them, they wished the mountains were on top of them to hide them. But he did not use all his strength, for he was not to destroy, but only to root them out of Heaven. He pushed them off into the bottomless pit.

Hell itself was frightened and would have fled, but Fate had bound her fast. Nine days the evil ones fell, confounding Chaos. Hell received them and closed over them. The Messiah went back to meet his saints who sang victory as he rode through Heaven to the temple of his Father.

Now, says Raphael, 893 ff., he has tried, by comparing heavenly things to earthly to give some idea of what happened. The point is, Satan envies man's state and plans to seduce him from obedience, so he can enslave him in eternal misery. That would give him revenge on God. Raphael urges Adam to warn Eve and not to sin. Both must profit by having heard of the terrible end of disobedience, 911 ff.,

> "Firm they might have stood,
> Yet fell; remember, and fear to transgress."

Commentary

Action precedes that of the first book of *Paradise Lost,* and relates events in Heaven before Satan fell. In accordance with the plan of the poem, Raphael turns the reference of the tale back to Adam to remind the reader where the scene is, and that he is comparing heavenly to earthly things. For example, he explains the assembling of God's armies in regular order, 73 ff.,

> "...as when the total kind
> Of Birds in orderly array on wing
> Came summoned over Eden to receive
> Their names of thee..."

When Milton reminds the reader of the difficulty of standing alone for what is right, and the hypocrisy of those who seem to be fair, he is talking from his experience in the civil war of England, his imprisonment, and his disillusionment with organized religion.

Again Milton enriches the poem with images. Of the sunrise, 3 ff.,

> "Waked by the circling Hours, with rosy hand
> Unbarred the gates of Light..."

He compares Satan's recoil from Abdiel's blow, 195 ff.,

> "...as if on Earth
> Winds under ground or waters forcing way
> Sidelong had pushed a Mountain from his seat,
> Half sunk with all his Pines..."

Speaking of the guns which toppled the good armies, Belial, good at double-meaning, says, 624 ff.,

> "...who receives them right,
> Had need from head to foot well understand;
> Not understood, this gift they have besides,
> They show us when our foes walk not upright."

BOOK SEVEN

Summary

Half way through his story, Milton opens, line 1, with another prayer to Urania for help to finish his story. He has fallen on evil times, that is blindness; but he does not feel alone so long as Urania visits him in his dreams, or at dawn. He prays that she will govern his song and find him an audience, though it may not be a large one.

The remainder of *Paradise Lost* concerns Earth. Milton asks Urania to tell him what happened after Raphael had warned Adam and Eve and charged them not to eat of the forbidden fruit.

Adam, 50 ff., amazed by the story of war in Heaven, wants to know, 70 ff., how Earth was made, and why and what had happened before he was created. He wants not to explore secrets, but to magnify God's works. He says there's enough time; even Sleep would listen to the story.

Raphael commends Adam, 111 ff., on his cautious request and says he will answer within bounds, and beyond that Adam must not ask. Knowledge, like food, can be overindulged. After Lucifer fell, God called the Son, 139 ff., and said that Heaven was yet populous enough, but he would repair the loss of fallen angels by creating a new race who by long obedience tried, could turn Earth into Heaven, one kingdom without end. The rest of the Heavenly powers might rest while the Son created the World.

Raphael explains, 174 ff., that creation took place at the Word of God, but in order to tell Adam he must use process of speech which will take time. All Heaven rejoiced that God was to make man a better race than the fallen angels. The Son chose his chariot, which also was spirit and of itself animated, and rode from the gate of Heaven. The Son told, 216 ff., the waters to be quiet, and the deep of Chaos to have peace. The rest of Heaven followed to see. The Son separated things favorable to life from those unfavorable and sent the latter downward. Then he formed like things to like and gathered them into a globe and in space hung the Earth.

The first day of creation the Son made light, 243 ff., and all the choirs of Heaven sang with joy. On the second day God made the firmament, 261 ff., to divide the waters above the Earth from those under the Earth, and again the choirs sang. On the third day, while all the warm oceans were urging the mother Earth to bring forth, God gathered the waters, 283 ff., into one place and let dry land appear. Like an army (and here Raphael reminds Adam that he has heard of armies, so perhaps he can understand what the angel is describing) the waters found their way. As soon as there was dry land, God told the Earth, 309 ff., to bring forth all sorts of green things. Immediately the Earth bloomed with vines, reeds, shrubs; and then the tall trees hung with blossoms and fruit; and all the Earth was watered with dew.

The fourth day, the sun, moon, and lesser lights were made,

339 ff., for ruling the day and night. The stars came from the cloudy shrine of pure light. The moon borrowed his light from the sun.

On the fifth day, 387 ff., the waters brought forth all sorts of living thing. The fowl flew above the Earth. The eggs hatched. The birds grew to full size and sang—all on that fifth day.

On the sixth day God made the animals, 451 ff., which came up from the Earth, 463 ff.,

> "...now half appeared
> The Tawny Lion, pawing to get free
> His hinder parts, then springs as broke from Bonds."

Raphael names and describes many of the animals. When all the Earth was done, there remained the creation of Man who would be master of Earth and worship God Supreme. God spoke to the Son, 519 ff.,
> "Let us make now Man in our image..."

God made man from the dust of the Earth and gave him dominion over all the Earth and charged him not to eat of the Tree of Knowledge of Good and Evil. Then on the Seventh day, the Son rested and all the heavens rejoiced while the choirs sang, 565 ff., and praised God's work.

Raphael finishes his story and asks Adam if he wants to know anything else.

Commentary
Milton again asks his muse for help. Since Urania is the muse of astronomy, she is heavenly compared to other muses. "In darkness" refers to Milton's blindness, and emphasizes his dependence on inner illumination which comes from Urania.

This section sketches creation week. Milton reminds the reader throughout the book that Raphael is telling the story to Adam. For example, he says creation was instantaneous, yet it will take time to put it into words. Although Adam's knowledge and experience are limited, Raphael tries to explain as in line 296 in an aside he says, "for of armies thou hast heard" and in line 561, speaking of heavenly choirs, he says, "thou remember'st, for thou heard'st."

One of the most striking figures is the creation of the lion quoted above. The reader can imagine blind Milton seeing with his inner eye all the pageantry of creation, enjoying images, painting them in vivid colors, 400 ff.,

> "Of Fish...sporting with quick glance
> Show to the Sun their waved coats dropped with Gold."

Milton has mentioned that Urania comes to him at dawn, and again the reader feels his joy in sunrise, 370 ff.,

> "First in his East the glorious Lamp was seen,
> Regent of Day, and all the Horizon round
> Invested with bright Rays, jocund to run
> His Longitude through Heaven's high road: the gray
> Dawn and the Pleiades before him danced,
> Shedding sweet influence."

Two examples of a favorite Milton usage, that is, use of an adjective for a noun, are: 267, "of this great round" for this great round earth and 368, "their small peculiar," meaning their small peculiar characteristic.

Milton believes in temperance even in acquiring knowledge, and has Adam approach it with caution.

BOOK EIGHT

Summary
Adam likes to hear the angel talk, and wants to keep him longer. He thanks the angel, 5 ff., for the information, but wants to know why all the heavenly bodies serve earth, when it seems such a waste for one World.

When Eve hears how the conversation is going, she goes out

into the garden; not that she isn't interested nor unable to comprehend, but she prefers to hear the story from Adam because he will
punctuate the story with caresses. This idealized description of
Eve, 40 ff., is followed by Milton's addressing the general public
to ask where they can find such marital love now. With line 59 he
continues about Eve's beauty.

Meanwhile, 66 ff., Raphael says he does not blame Adam for
wanting to know, but that whether Heaven or Earth move about
each other is not important, and there are some things that God
has left concealed — some things unknown so He could laugh at the
peculiar opinions that men would have thereafter when they tried
to figure out the heavens.

And Raphael says he thinks from the way Adam's mind works,
that Adam's children will be very curious about the heavens. But
why the brighter serves the apparently lesser is not for Adam to
ponder. And "great or bright infers not excellence." Why not think
that God built with such a magnificent hand that man would realize
that the World was too large for him? It is good that God places
some things above understanding. Then the angel asks various
questions about what might be — perhaps the Earth moves to meet
the sun. He advises Adam to leave all that to God and enjoy
what he has.

Adam thanks the angel for explaining, 192 ff.,

> "............to know
>   That which before us lies in daily life,
>   Is the prime Wisdom..."

But Adam wants to detain the angel so he asks him to listen while
Adam tells what he remembers of his own creation.

Raphael answers, 218 ff., that Adam need not apologize for his
speech, that God has given him many gifts and those in Heaven
don't think those of Earth beneath them, but fellow-servants.
Heavenly beings see that Man has God's equal love. He urges
Adam to tell his story because Raphael on the day of Adam's

creation was guarding Hell so that none might come out to spy. The gates of Hell were fast shut; but within were loud lamentations and rage.

Adam begins, 250 ff., with how he waked from sound sleep to find himself lying on flowery herbs, wet with balmy sweat. The sun soon dried him off, and he looked at Heaven and wished he might spring upward. He stood, looked around, and wondered who he was. He tried to speak and found he could talk and could name whatever he saw. First he asked the sun, 273 ff., for identification. He felt he was happier than he could comprehend.

No one answered his plea so he sat down on a green bank and fell into a gentle sleep. At first he thought he was going to dissolve into nothing, his former state; but a figure stood at his head and talked to him. The heavenly shape said, 296 ff., that Adam should come to the mansion awaiting him. He called Adam the first man, the first father. The shape took Adam and flew with him through the air. They looked down on fields and waters, alighting in a garden more beautiful than anything Adam had seen. The wonderful fruit made him hungry; he woke and found his dream a reality. He would have wandered again, had not the Divine Presence appeared. Adam fell at his feet, but the Presence lifted him and said, 316, "Whom thou sought'st I am."

The Divine One said that all the garden was Adam's. He might eat of all but the Tree of Knowledge of Good and Evil. If he disobeyed in this, he would die.

These words made Adam afraid and he resolved to follow divine direction. The Being said, 338 ff., he was giving Adam and his descendants all the Earth and its inhabitants. He brought all living things (except the fish who couldn't come) to Adam to be named.

God endowed Adam with sudden knowledge. Adam asked the Heavenly Visitor's name, 357 ff., that he might worship. He added that he did not see anyone in Paradise with whom he could hold communion, and asked who could enjoy solitude.

The Vision answered, 369 ff., by asking what solitude was. There were many creatures on Earth, whom Adam understood. Animals could know and reason to a certain extent. He advised Adam to find happiness in ruling these.

Adam thought this was God's final word, and he implored forgiveness for speaking, 379 ff. He explained that if he were God's substitute on Earth and if the animals were inferior, how could he commune with them? He wanted rational companionship. A lion lived with a lioness, but the kinds did not mix, and man least of all could have companionship with beasts.

God, pleased with Adam's argument, 399 ff., teased him further by saying that God lived alone and that he had communication only with inferiors, for he had no equals.

Adam answered, 412 ff., that nobody could understand God, Who is Perfect. God had no need to propagate for he is infinite. He could raise any creature up to the degree where he could communicate with it. But man, if he were to multiply, needed a companion; for Adam by his own power, couldn't raise a beast erect to talk with him.

God said, 437 ff., that he was testing Adam's free spirit. He knew that it was not good for man to live alone, and he would fill Adam's desire.

Then Adam fell into a sleep, but he seemed to understand what was going on and realized that God took a rib and fashioned it into a creature so lovely that everything else seemed commonplace. Adam waked determined to find her or mourn forever. He had about given up, when he saw her being led to him by her Heavenly Maker, though unseen. God gave her to Adam and Adam said, 491 ff., that she fulfilled everything he wanted. Because she came from man, she should be Woman and the two should be one.

Eve heard him and Nature taught her to be modest so that Adam had to win her and lead her blushing into their bower. All the Earth congratulated them, 513 ff.,

> "...........the Earth
> Gave sign of gratulation, and each Hill;
> Joyous the Birds; fresh Gales and gentle Airs
> Whispered it to the Woods, and from their wings
> Flung Rose, flung Odors from the spicy Shrub,
> Disporting, til the amorous Bird of Night
> Sung spousal, and bid haste the evening star
> On his hill top, to light the bridal lamp."

Adam tells Raphael that nothing compares to marital bliss. He knows that Eve is by nature inferior in mind and inward powers, but that outwardly she is greater. Adam says when he approaches Eve, she seems absolute in herself, 551 ff.,

> "All higher knowledge in her presence falls
> Degraded, Wisdom in discourse with her
> Loses discountenanced, and like folly shows;
> Authority and Reason on her wait,
> As one intended first, not after made...."

Adam's attitude disturbs the angel and he counsels him, 561 ff., not to blame Nature for making Eve so fair, and not to give things more due than is their worth. He is to love Eve but not be subject to her. Wisdom will help him if he doesn't desert it. If he values himself, Eve will value him more. If physical passion is such delight, remember that all the animals have the same and if it were such a powerful thing, worthy to conquer the soul of man, it wouldn't have been given the beasts. Love is fine; passion is not. True love will help him ascend to heavenly love; and if love were only carnal pleasure, Adam could have found a mate among the beasts.

Adam, taken back a little, answers, 596 ff., that although physical love is great, it does not matter so much as all the little daily acts of sweetness and harmony that makes marriage so wonderful. He is just telling the angel his feelings, not his actions. And if love leads up to Heaven, do heavenly spirits love and if so, how?

The angel blushes and says, 620 ff.,
> "...Let it suffice thee that thou know'st
> Us happy, and without Love no happiness."

Whatever man enjoys, the angels enjoy without obstacle. Then the angel says it is getting late and near sun set. He must go; but he advises Adam to be strong, live happy, love, but first of all obey God, and not let passion sway his judgment. In Adam lies the fate of all his sons; and Heaven will rejoice in his steadfastness; but to stand or fall lies in Adam's own free will.

Adam says, 645 ff., that he is grateful for the visit and the message and invites the angel to return often. The two part. The angel ascends to Heaven, and Adam enters his bower.

Commentary

This section concerns itself with the dignity of man and his place as ruler of the Earth. The sun and heavenly bodies make the Earth a fit place for man and his children. In itself the sun is barren and comes to fruition only on earth. Compare this with III, 586, "invisible virtue" of the sun. For Milton light or the sun symbolizes Good.

When newly-created Adam wakens, his natural impulse is upward. This repeats what Moloch has said, II, 75, that the proper motion of spirits is upward. Adam knows he is more than animal, needs a proper mate.

Eve's natural impulse is to let Adam rule her, though Adam (and here the cards are stacked against him from the start) is overcome by her beauty. This foreshadows the fall; for Adam says higher knowledge falls in Eve's presence. The angel tells Adam this is passion, not love. And it is passion, not ignorance which causes Adam to choose Eve rather than obedience.

At the reproof of the angel, Adam cleverly turns the tables and asks the angel about love in heaven, whereat the angel blushes, and reveals only that they love.

Milton had three marriages, and he has his opinion on marriage, on what women ought to be and how men ought to feel about them. Although the women of Milton's day were not thought worthy of education, Milton, agreeing that they are inferior, thinks they are of great value when subject to their husbands.

BOOK NINE

Summary

At the beginning of Book Nine, Milton talks to the reader, 1 ff. He can speak no more of God's visiting man, because the story becomes tragic; but it is a story more worthy to be told than the *Iliad,* the *Odyssey* or the *Aeneid.*

Milton will tell the story if his "celestial patroness" continues to come nightly and give him his verses. He has not been interested in wars, doesn't want to sing of them, but he has taken a long time to choose his subject, and he is late beginning. If the Muse doesn't help him, his song will be wrong, coming in an age too late, a climate too cold; or years will wither his intended flight into song.

He continues the story, 48 ff. The sun has set and Satan spends the night flying around the Earth, looking things over. Finally, he rises with the river mist just under the Tree of Life, and chooses the serpent as the best disguise, because the wily serpent might not arouse suspicion if he did witty and subtle things.

But before he enters the serpent, Satan looks around and mourns, 99 ff., how like to Heaven is Earth, more beautiful even, because God had the experience of his first building. Satan knows what delight he could have had walking about Earth. The more pleasures he sees possible, the worse his torment. Good becomes evil to him. He states his purpose, 126 ff.,

> "Nor hope to be myself less miserable
> By what I seek, but others to make such
> As I...."

He hopes in one day to spoil what God has done in six. He claims to have freed in one night half the angels. He thinks perhaps God didn't have virtue to create more angels; or maybe he made man of earth and gave him all the heavenly spoils just to spite Satan. Afraid of angels who might be guarding Eden, Satan looks for the serpent, and sees himself debased into bestial slime, incarnating into a brute his own essence that had aspired to be a god, 171 ff.,

> "...........Revenge, at first though sweet,
> Bitter ere long back on itself recoils;
> Let it; I reck not, so it light well aimed,
> Since higher I fall short, on him who next
> Provokes my envy, this new Favorite
> Of Heaven, this Man of Clay, Son of despite,
> Whom us the more to spite his Maker raised
> From dust: spite then with spite is best repaid."

Satan finishes his soliloquy and creeps like black mist, goes in at the serpent's mouth and does not disturb his sleep, waiting for dawn.

At daybreak Adam and Eve come out and pray aloud, joining all things silent or otherwise in worship. They discuss the day's work, and Eve says, 205 ff., that until there are more hands to help, the work is too much. If they are together, they waste time talking and caressing, therefore they should work apart.

Adam doesn't like this idea. He says, 227 ff., that God didn't intend work to be a burden, that love is not the lowest end of human life. He could let her go for a little while; but he is afraid that harm will come to her. They have been warned of their vicious foe; and if he finds them apart, he will have the advantage. He implores her not to leave his protection.

Hurt, Eve replies, 273 ff., that Adam doesn't trust her. She knows they have a foe; but why should Adam doubt her fidelity? They need not fear violence, since they are incapable of death or pain. If Adam fears she will be a victim of fraud, he just doesn't trust her.

Adam assures her, 291 ff., that he doesn't doubt her, but he doesn't want her insulted by the devil. He wouldn't dare anything if they were together. Why should she choose her trial when Adam is absent?

Eve persists, 322 ff., that if they are afraid, they aren't happy, 335 ff.,

> "And what is Faith, Love, Virtue, unassayed
> Alone, without exterior help sustained?"

If each of them can't stand alone, their happiness is frail and Eden isn't Eden.

Adam answers, 343 ff., that everything is perfect, but, 348 ff.,

> "...........within himself
> The danger lies, yet lies within his power:
> Against his will he can receive no harm."

That which obeys reason is free; but something might appear fair and so deceive, since reason can be deceived. He asks her not to seek temptation, approve first her obedience. But, if she is determined to go, go, for staying against her will makes her more absent. He charges her that God has done his part, she must do hers.

Eve answers, 378 ff., that with his permission, she will go warned because he has suggested they may be less prepared than they think. She doesn't think a proud foe will try first to conquer the weaker.

Eve departs, more graceful than any goddess described in classic literature. Adam watches her, wishes she would not go, charges her to hurry back. She promises to return by noon.

Here Milton breaks in, 404 ff., with a mournful lament for Eve who will never return innocent. He tells how since dawn the Devil, in the form of a serpent has looked for Adam and Eve, hoping to find Eve alone, but doubting that he will. Then he sees her, a fair unsupported flower binding up other flowers. By classical allusion Milton paints Paradise as more wonderful than any described in literature.

Satan admires Eve, and for a time forgets his horrible mission, and sits there "stupidly good." Then he recalls his hate and spite, and speaks to himself, 473 ff., wondering how his thoughts have made him forget hate. He has come to destroy pleasure. His only joy will be in destruction. He must not lose this opportunity while Adam is absent. He shuns Adam's greater strength, for he realizes that Sin and Hell have enfeebled him, 489 ff.,

> "She fair, divinely fair, fit Love for Gods,
> Not terrible, though terror be in Love
> And beauty, not approached by stronger hate,
> Hate stronger, under shew of Love well feigned..."

The serpent goes toward Eve; and he is of a lovely shape and color, more beautiful than any serpents of mythology. Eve pays no attention to him, as she is accustomed to animals around her. He plays so long she finally looks at him. He talks, 532 ff., and asks her pardon for looking at her, the fairest of all, who has only one man (and what is one?) to adore her when she should be a goddess, served by angels numberless.

Thus Satan flatters her. Amazed she asks, 533 ff., how he has a voice, since she had thought beasts were mute, and how does it happen he is so devoted to her?

Satan answers, 568 ff., that at first he was like other animals and knew nothing but food and sex. One day he ate of a certain fruit, wonderful apples, and he found alteration in himself, reason and speech, though his shape remained. Then he considered everything in Heaven or Earth or between and found Eve the most beautiful and worthy of worship.

Off guard, Eve answers, 615 ff., that his lavish praise makes her doubt the virtue of the fruit, but she wants to know where the fruit is for there are many trees whose fruit they have not tried.

Triumphant, the serpent offers, 626 ff., to lead her, the Empress, to the place. Eve tells him to go; and she follows as one follows a will of the wisp. When she sees the tree, she says, 647 ff., that he might have saved their time, as this is the forbidden tree.

The tempter asks, 656 ff., if that is really so, and Eve answers, 659 ff., they may eat of any other, but if they eat of this, they shall surely die.

The snake pretends to be indignant about this deprivation and acts very emotional, moving its body this way and that in agitation, like some classical orator preparing to speak. The Devil says, 679 ff., he feels the wisdom of the tree in him, that she should not fear death, that she won't die by eating the fruit for it gives life. He has eaten and did not die; neither will she. He has attained a more perfect state by "venturing higher than my lot." Should beast have more advantage than man? God will praise her courage. And what is evil? Ought she not to know so she can shun it? A just God can't punish her. He wants his worshippers low and ignorant. If she eats, she will be as a god, since he, a beast, ate it and is human. She, now a human, will be a god.

Perhaps death is merely putting off being human and becoming a god. Satan says he sees the Earth producing, but he sees the gods doing nothing. What is wrong with knowing? What can they learn against God's will, if all be His? Maybe God is envious. He then addresses her as a goddess and begs her to eat.

She listens, looks at the fruit, and since it is noon, she is hungry. She rationalizes, 745 ff., by addressing the Tree of Knowledge of Good and Evil saying it must be good for it taught the mute to speak. Whoever named it the Tree of Knowledge knew it to be good, and its being forbidden commends it more, since it forbids them to be wise. The serpent did not die. Is death for man only, when he eats? The one beast who has eaten is friendly to man, not deceitful. She asks herself what she is afraid of and reaches for the fruit.

All nature revolts at the sin, and even the guilty serpent slinks back to his thicket. At first greedy Eve is interested only in eating. She praises the tree, 795 ff., which can confer wisdom. She vows to tend first each morning the Tree of Knowledge until she grows mature in wisdom like the gods. Then she praises experience without which she wouldn't have eaten. Maybe God, the Great Forbidder, has not seen her eat. Should she tell Adam or should she use the secret to become superior to him? But if she should die and Adam have another wife — the thought is unbearable, 831 ff.,

> "Adam shall share with me in bliss or woe:
> So dear I love him, that with him all deaths
> I could endure, without him live no life."

Before leaving she bows in homage to the Tree. Meanwhile, Adam waits for her, has woven a garland for her, but he is worried so he starts to look for her. He finds her near the Tree, with fruit in her hand. Her face begs excuse. She says, 856 ff., that she will never again leave his side, but strange things have happened. The Tree is not a tree of danger. The serpent has eaten and grown to human. She has eaten and is growing to godhead. Chiefly, she says, she wants the knowledge and godhead for Adam, and she urges him to eat lest she want to put off her Deity later and can't.

Adam sees what she has done, the distemper in her cheek, and he is speechless with horror. He wonders, 896 ff., how a creature so beautiful and holy can be lost, marked for death. Through fraud of the enemy she is ruined, and Adam also, for he can't live without her. Another Eve from another rib wouldn't do.

Having decided, he seems more calm and tells Eve, 921 ff., that she has been bold, but perhaps God won't destroy them, and have the Enemy say He is fickle. Perhaps they will learn more. In any case, Adam chooses to go with Eve.

Eve thanks Adam, 961 ff., for this trial of his love, which she wouldn't have otherwise known. If she thought death were really coming she'd face it alone, but she thinks life opens for her. This fruit makes everything else taste flat. She urges Adam not to fear, but to eat.

She hugs him, cries because he will risk divine displeasure and death for her. She gives him fruit and against his better judgment, he eats it. He is not deceived, but overcome with Eve's charm.

Earth trembles; Nature groans; the sky weeps at the completion of mortal sin; but Adam and Eve pay no attention. They eat, laugh, imagine they are growing wings. And their passion which was so pure, changes to lust. Adam says, 1017 ff., they have been missing much by not eating of the forbidden fruit, and asks Eve to come make love. She seems more desirable than ever.

They go, passion their mutual guilt. Finally worn out with passion, they sleep. When the first effect of the fruit has gone, they wake to disillusionment. They know nakedness and shame. Shame covering them only makes them more naked. Finally Adam bewails the evil hour, 1067 ff., when Eve listened to the false worm. They now know good lost and evil gained, and their faces show it. How can he ever look at God or angel again? Wishing to hide, he suggests they find some cover for their shame.

They find fig-leaves, even as Columbus found the Indians with a feathered belt. Once covered, Adam and Eve sit down to cry, while passions rage: anger, hate and all evil states where once had been peace. Now Will and Understanding are slaves to sensual Appetite. Adam bemoans Eve, 1134 ff., for not having listened to him that morning. He hints she was already then failing in obedience.

Offended by being blamed, Eve asks, 1144 ff., if he is saying it couldn't have happened to both of them or to him alone, so wily was the serpent and Eve no reason to think he would harm her. If Eve couldn't leave his side, she had better stayed a rib. Anyhow, since Adam knew she was weak, he should have commanded her to stay with him, but no, he had practically sent her to sin.

Now Adam asks in anger, 1163 ff., if this is his reward for choosing death with her. Now it's all his fault. This is what happens whan a man lets a woman have her way, but otherwise he would have had to use force, and if one uses force, how can there be free will? So each blames the other.

Commentary

This, the longest book of the twelve, shows Milton's knowledge of human nature. Satan claims to have liberated one-half of the angels, but Raphael, V. 710, has said one-third. Eve, determined to have her own way about working separately, tells Adam she leaves with his permission, which he has not given. Later she blames him for letting her go. Adam has said, 372, "Go; for thy stay, not free, absents thee more..." Adam defends his action as in keeping with free will.

Satan tempts Eve with the same temptation for which he fell: desire to be worshipped. She has only one man to admire her, and what is one? When Adam follows Eve, he allows passion to rule him, just as the angel has feared.

Milton presents Eve as a clever, fascinating and deceptive creature. She mocks the serpent when he overpraises her, saying she doubts the wisdom of the fruit, since his praise is so extravagant, but she is pleased. When Eve sins, she is hungry and deceived by the persuasive serpent, but her transgression lies in physical appetite and greed. After sinning, she reacts in the opposite way from what she has done before. She exhibits selfishness, jealousy, idolatry. She lies about her reason for eating the fruit, saying she wanted godhead for Adam, when she has really decided to take Adam with her one way or another.

Adam's decision to go with Eve is based on passion. He rationalizes his sin just as Eve has done, 921 ff.

Their domestic quarrel no doubt echoes Milton's own household troubles. In a burst of self-pity Adam calls the tempting snake that "false worm."

At the beginning of Book Nine, Milton restates his theme that tasting the Tree brought death, Compare 1, 2, 3 and IX, II. He also repeats the idea that the danger lies in man himself, 348-9.

The fig leaves that Adam and Eve used are from the Indian banyan tree, but Milton was mistaken about their size.

Outstanding figures in this book are, 424 ff.,

"........Eve separate he spies,
....
Herself, though fairest unsupported Flower,
From her best prop so far, and storm so nigh."

and, 499 ff.,

"........his Head
Crested aloft, and Carbuncle his Eyes;
With burnished Neck of verdant Gold, erect
Amidst his circling Spires, that on the grass
Floated redundant..."

The carbuncle eyes are red, symbolizing passion. Later after the fall, Eve's eyes dart contagious fire, also symbolizing passion.

BOOK TEN

Summary

Man's sin is known in Heaven. Milton observes, 9 ff., that man had strength and free will to resist, and therefore deserved to fall. The story continues with the angel guard hurrying to Heaven to explain they have been vigilant, and to ask forgiveness for not keeping Satan out of Paradise. Everyone runs to hear their story, and then the Father says, 34 ff., that they couldn't prevent it. He knew it would happen. He did not decree that man should fall, but he did not stop it. Now that he is fallen, sentence must be given. Man thinks because the sentence hasn't been given, that he will not die. God tells the Son that he, who will redeem man, must pass the sentence.

The Son says, 68 ff., he will go, but whatever judgment given will eventually fall on Him. He will temper justice with mercy so as to satisfy both man and God. He wants no angels with him. He will judge only the two, Adam and Eve. Satan will be absent. As for the serpent, it is not to blame.

The Son rises from his throne and all the angels go with him to Heaven's gate, where they look down on Eden. The Son speeds downward. It is the afternoon of the day in which they have sinned. They hear the Voice of God and are afraid and hide.

The Son calls to ask where they are and why they don't come, as usual, to meet him. Adam and Eve, much ashamed, full of hate and guilt, come. Adam says he is afraid because he is naked. The Son asks him who told him he is naked and has he eaten of the fruit?

Adam answers, 125 ff., that he doesn't know what to say — whether to blame himself or Eve, but he ends up blaming Eve and God because he gave Eve to Adam.

The Son asks, 145 ff., if Eve was his god to obey. She was to be in subjection to Adam, not the other way, and Adam should have ruled. He asks Eve what she has done, and she blames the serpent. Then the Son curses the serpent, although he is actually cursing Satan when he says the seed of the woman will bruise the Serpent's head while the Serpent will only bruise the heel of man. Here Milton interrupts to say that this prophecy was fulfilled in Christ's overcoming of Satan.

The Son continues judgment on the woman, saying she shall bring forth children in pain and be subject to her husband. As for Adam, he will eat in sorrow, and work hard to gain his bread until he dies.

So He judges them, removing death to a distant time, and seeing how they shiver in the air already changing to winter, He clothes them in skins of beasts. He covers their inner nakedness with His robe of righteousness. He then returns to Heaven to report and plead for man.

Meanwhile at the gates of Hell sit Sin and Death. Sin tells her son Death, 235 ff., that she feels things are going well for Satan. She wants to go to Earth, but first they should build a broad road, a monument to Evil, so there will be no inconvenience in passage between the new World and Hell.

Death answers, 265 ff., that he will be happy to go with her, that he smells the carnage he will devour. He snuffs the "smell Of mortal change on Earth" just like a vulture, who in a battlefield waits for corpses. Sin and Death build a road to Earth, greater than any vaunted earth bridges, so that they join Hell and Earth. Sin and Death are just going into Paradise when they meet Satan, disguised as a bright angel, but they recognize him.

After he had seduced Eve, he had sneaked into the woods and changed shape to see what happened, but when he saw the Son coming to judge them, he had fled, and then come back at night to listen to Adam and Eve lament. Satan is jubilant over the fall, over his children Sin and Death, and the bridge they have built.

Sin tells her father, 354 ff., that she knew by the secret harmony between them that he had prospered, and that Hell could no longer hold them. They are here to see the monarchy of God divided with Satan, for he will rule the World.

Satan compliments them, 384 ff., on their good work of making Earth and Hell one realm. They are his true children. He wants them to enter the World, make man their slave and then kill him. They are to represent Satan. If they do well, Hell never need fear. He bids them "go and be strong."

As they go on their way, even the stars are blasted and turn pale. Satan goes down toward Hell, where Chaos surges against the bridge, but can't move it. Satan enters Hell, finds everyone sitting around waiting for his return. He goes through the crowd like an ordinary angel, and they don't know him. Invisible, he sits on the throne but finally allows his false glitter to shine through, and all are amazed and happy.

Satan says, 460 ff., he has been successful beyond hope, that they are lords of a World, little inferior to Heaven, that there is a new highway to Earth, made by Sin and Death. He tells how hard the first journey to Paradise was, how he seduced Man with an apple. He thinks this very funny. He says they may now rule Man, and that judgment also has been said on him, that the seed of man should bruise his head. But the time for this is not set, and who would not endure a bruise for such a World as he has gained? He calls them to go up and enter bliss.

Satan expects them to applaud, but all he hears is a dismal universal hiss, and then he feels himself turning into a snake. All the snakes hiss and writhe together. Outside, some of the fallen angels are waiting the exit of the group with Satan at their head. They are amazed to see a mass of snakes tumble out, and then they feel themselves also turning into snakes. A grove of fruit like the Tree of Knowledge of Good and Evil springs up; and the snakes, starving, eat the fruit, only to have it turn to cinders and bitter ashes in their mouths. This they do over and over, repeating Eve's sin, unable to stop themselves.

Finally they are permitted their original shape, but there is a legend that they must turn into snakes once a year to humble themselves.

Meanwhile Sin and Death arrive in Paradise. Sin asks Death what he thinks of their empire, 591 ff. Isn't it better than sitting in Hell half-starved? Death says, 597 ff., that he is always hungry, and it doesn't matter where he is, just so he has enough to eat. Though Earth looks plenteous, it seems too little to fill his "vast unhidebound corpse."

Sin tells him, 603 ff., to feed on the herbs and fruits and flowers, next on beasts, fish, and fowl, and whatever Time gives him, until Sin lives in man long enough to infect and season him; and then he can be Death's "last and sweetest prey." Sin and Death go separate ways to destroy and pollute God's creation.

God sees all this and says, 616 ff., they are his Hell hounds, whom man's folly has let in. They won't know that God called them to act as scavengers, until they are so stuffed with offal that at one stroke of his arm, the Son can cast all of them into Hell and seal up the gates. Until that time, let them go on. The curse is upon them.

Then the heavenly chorus sings hallelujah, saying God's way is just. God tells various angels to change the sun so there will be extremes of climate, and to make the moon shine with noxious efficacy, and the stars to join in malignant influence. He resets the winds to bluster and some say he turned the poles of the Earth to make the axle oblique, else there had always been spring.

The elements now turn unfriendly and man experiences outrage from lifeless things. Discord, daughter of Sin, has caused quarreling between beast and beast and between fowl and fowl, so that they devour each other and fear man. Adam sees these growing miseries around him, but his inner conflict is even worse.

He laments the situation, 720 ff., and wishes for death. He does not want children who will curse him for bringing them into this mess. He tells God, 743 ff., he didn't ask to be made; therefore he ought to be dissolved back to dust. He tells himself, 756 ff., he shouldn't have accepted God's conditions. But in all fairness he should not accept the good and then complain about the bad. Suppose he himself had a son who was disobedient and who asked his father why he was born. Would Adam accept such a statement from his own son? Then he thinks a son might be born to him not by choice but by necessity. But God had a choice, and the punishment is justly at God's will, and Adam is willing to die any minute. But why doesn't death hurry? He wants to lie down and hear no more, and have no offspring.

Then he is afraid that dying might not be eternal, that he might know a living death and suffer forever. He wonders about the nature of man and what might survive. Can God make death deathless? Maybe death is endless misery from then onward—as he now feels it is. He is afraid both Death and he will be found eternal. Then his sons ought to curse him. At last he absolves God and takes all the blame. He feels himself kin only to Satan, the weight of evil more than he can bear, even though his wicked wife shares it.

So Adam laments, feeling the night sinister where before it was friendly. He lies on the cold ground and longs for Death. Eve, feeling just as desolate, speaks to him; but he calls her a serpent, 867 ff., and blames her for everything. If it had not been for her pride, vanity, and "longing to be seen Though by the Devil himself," a "Rib Crooked by nature," they would not have fallen. He blames God for giving Earth this fair "defect." Why didn't he create all men and no women and find another way to propagate mankind? He blames it all on sex and says man will never find happiness in love, that something will always be wrong.

Eve pleads with him, saying she didn't mean to offend him, that she needs his strength, that maybe they have only an hour to live and there should be peace between them. He has sinned only against God, but she has sinned against both God and Adam, and the whole blame is hers, and she wants all the punishment.

As she cries, Adam relents because he really loves her. He says, 947 ff., that she couldn't bear all the punishment, since she can't even bear his displeasure. If prayers could alter the decree, he would speed to ask that all be on his head, but they should see how they can help each other; because he thinks death will be a "slow-paced evil, A long day's dying," and pain to their children.

Eve says, 967 ff., that she knows he won't listen to her, but she thinks they might kill themselves. They could remain childless, or if this is impossible, then they can see Death and destroy destruction with destruction.

Adam comforts her, 1013 ff., saying that Death might not exempt them from pain, and they can't cheat their destiny. God would make death live in them. He recalls the promise that the woman's seed would bruise the head of the serpent. That will be revenge, and for that they must have children. He reminds her that God was kind when he passed sentence, and that he told her she would endure pain in childbearing and that Adam must work hard. He thinks idleness would have been worse. He reminds Eve that God clothed them, and if they pray, God will show them how to deal with the inclement seasons, and perhaps how to make fire. God will help them make their lives endurable. He thinks they should go back to the place where God judged them and there confess and pray. God will hear.

They agree, go to the place, fall down and confess, asking pardon and crying in sorrow and humiliation.

Commentary

The action in this book moves from Heaven to Earth, from Earth to Hell and back.

Milton poses the question of foreknowledge versus predestination in God's statement that the angels couldn't have prevented Satan's entrance into Paradise nor the fall of man. God calls Sin and Death his Hell Hounds. Milton thinks foreknowledge (knowledge of the event before it happens) can be independent of predestination (causing the event to happen). He is careful to emphasize man's free will, responsibility, and dignity. If man were to have free will and god-like intelligence, he would sometimes make the wrong choice.

In the lamentations of the unhappy Adam and Eve, the reader no doubt benefits from Milton's own stormy domestic life. Adam's regret that God ever made woman, is perhaps Milton's own regret that his young wife left him and would not return nor would the church grant divorce. One can almost hear Adam complaining of a woman who wanted to be seen, though by the Devil himself.

Adam shows all the mental agony of a man in despair: Why was I born? Why can't I die? Is death the end? Maybe there is something worse? As for women, Adam is sure that man will never find a fit mate, only someone misfortune or mistake brings him. Or the one he wants will refuse out of perverseness, only to marry someone worse. Or if she loves him, her parents will forbid the marriage, or perhaps he will meet his love too late and find her already married to some enemy. He declares woman the cause of infinite calamity.

Yet, bad as women fare in the lament of Adam, Eve shows more devotion than he in her offer to die and to take all the blame for their trouble. It is she who tries to make up to Adam, admitting her fault.

BOOK ELEVEN

Summary

Adam and Eve pray, 1ff., since God has softened their hearts, for the salvation of mankind. Their prayers go straight to Heaven where the Son wraps them in incense and brings them to God.

The Son intercedes, 22 ff., saying that these are the first fruits of his implanted Grace in man, more sweet than all those fruits in Paradise which man tended before he fell. The Son asks that man may live reconciled until through the sacrifice of the Son, man may live again in Heaven.

The Father grants all, 46 ff., that the Son asks, but man may no longer live in Paradise. Nature's law will not allow it. God had given man happiness and immortality; and for him to eat of the Tree of Life now, would only make his woe eternal, for death will be his final remedy, and after death will come second life. Then God says that since the blest through Heaven have seen his dealings with fallen angels, they should also hear his judgments on man.

The trumpet brings everyone to God's throne. God says, 84 ff., that man has now become like the gods, for he knows both good and evil. He would have been happier to have remained ignorant of evil, but now that his variable mind is known, God thinks it best that he not eat of the Tree of Life and live forever, or dream that he will live forever. Michael is to go down with the Cherubim (lest Satan bother him) and drive out the pair from Paradise, and tell them something of the future.

Adam and Eve will scarcely be able to bear this sentence, so God says to hide all terror and let them have hope, and to reveal to Adam the fulfillment of the prophecy of the wounding of the Serpent. They are to leave a guard of flame over Paradise lest it become a place for foul spirits.

While the Archangel is preparing to go down, dawn comes and

finds Adam and Eve, their prayers finished, with new hope. Adam says, 141 ff., that it is easy to believe that good comes from Heaven, but hard to think that anything man sends upward could concern the mind of God. But prayer or even a sigh, reaches God. Adam thinks that since he kneeled and prayed with humble heart, he has seen God listening with kindness. Adam begins to believe he has been heard. Peace has returned to his heart and he remembers the promise that Eve's seed would bruise the foe. He had forgotten this for a moment, but now he is sure the bitterness of death is past, that they shall live. And through Eve man shall live and all things live for man. He calls her "Mother of all Mankind."

Eve answers, 163 ff., that she is not worthy to such honor because it is all her fault, and she ought not to be trusted, but God has given her the greatest honor of all. First God forgives her; then Adam gives her a title she doesn't deserve. Now they must go to work; they are doomed to toil, but what can be toil in this lovely place? She will never stray again from his side, and they will work content, though fallen.

But Fate will not permit them to stay in Paradise. Nature first gives signs. The air darkens soon after dawn; an eagle drives two other birds before him; a beast pursues a pair of deer toward the eastern gate. Adam sees these portents and says, 193 ff., that further change is coming, and that Heaven is trying to tell them not to feel too secure, they are but dust. Morning light comes from a cloud in the west while the east lies dark.

By now the heavenly band has alighted on a hill in Paradise; but Adam's eyes, darkened by sin, see only a cloud of light, from which comes a Heavenly Being. Adam describes him, 226 ff., as not terrible nor sociable, but "solemn and sublime." Eve must retire while Adam meets him with reverence.

Michael comes as a man, though clothed in rainbow colors, and says, 251 ff., that Adam's prayers are heard and Death will be postponed, with days wherein he may repent. God will redeem him, but he may not stay in Paradise.

Adam is stricken at the news; and Eve, out of sight, laments, 268 ff., that this is worse than death to leave the happy walks and such fond memories, and the little home she has adorned. How can she breathe in a different air?

The angel tells Eve, 287 ff., not to grieve over losing what they have justly lost. Adam will be with her; and wherever they both are, that will be home.

Then Adam, pulling himself together says to Michael, 296 ff., that he has been gentle in telling them what would otherwise have killed them. If prayer could help, Adam would never cease; but there is no use praying against God's absolute decree. Adam submits but thinks that if they leave Paradise they will never see God's face again, nor worship in places where God has been. Neither can he tell his sons that God walked there and that Adam heard his voice. Nor can he put up altars. He asks, 328 ff.,

> "In yonder nether World where shall I seek
> His bright appearances, or footstep trace?"

From sin and revolt, Adam has returned to adoration.

Michael says, 335 ff., that God is everywhere. Adam must not think God's presence confined to any narrow bounds. Perhaps Paradise might have been the capitol, but now Adam must live on lower ground with his sons. But he will find God there, will feel God's love. But before Adam leaves Paradise, he is to hear what will happen in future days and years. Adam will learn patience and moderation, in order that he can endure mortal life and face Death when it comes. Meanwhile, Eve is to sleep, but her rest will also be instructive, as Adam's was when Eve was formed.

Adam answers, 371 ff., that he is ready for whatever may come so that he may come to final rest. They go into a hill of Paradise and see all the Earth, but this is not higher nor wider than the pinnace wherein Satan tempts Christ with views of the World's kingdoms. Here follows a list of all the possible places they could have seen. Michael purges Adam's eyes and mind from the cloud of sin, gives him three drops of the well of life, which makes Adam fall into a trance, but the angel raises him up and says, 423 ff., that he should look and see what sin has done to those who never touched the tree nor had anything to do with the Snake. Adam sees Cain and Abel, offering sacrifices. Abel's lamb is accepted, Cain's grain is not. Angry, Cain kills his brother.

Adam cries out that it is not fair that the devout and meek man should be hurt. Michael answers, 454 ff., that these are Adam's sons, that the unjust has killed the just for envy, but that the good one's faith will be rewarded, although Adam sees only his death.

Then Adam says, 461 ff., that he has now seen death. Is this the way we die? How horrible!

Michael answers, 466 ff., that this is death, but death comes in many shapes—all dismal. Causes may be fire, flood, famine, but more often intemperance, the sin of Eve. Then Adam sees a pest house where all sorts of sick people writhe in agony. Despair tends the beds and Death shakes his dart but delays striking, although man begs for him. Adam cries, but finally gets control of himself and says, 500 ff., that it would be better for them to die unborn. Why have life if it must end like this? Can God's image in man be subjected to this? Why, if he is made in God's image, can't man be exempt from this suffering?

Michael answers, 515 ff., that when they gave themselves to "ungoverned appetite" they forsook God's image. So abject is their punishment they disfigure themselves because they did not reverence God in themselves. Adam admits this punishment is just, but inquires if there isn't a better way to die.

Michael says, 530 ff., that if a man follows the rule of "Not too much" in eating, drinking, and all things, many years will he live and return to mother earth like a ripe fruit dropping, mature for death. This is old age, and if one meet death this way, he must lose his strength and beauty of youth. His senses will lose the taste of pleasure, and a damp melancholy will weigh the spirits in old age and "Consume The Balm of Life."

To this Adam says, 547 ff., that he won't avoid death, nor try to prolong life, but watch how he may be easiest rid of the charge of life, which he will have to keep until his appointed time.

The angel answers, 553 ff.,

> "Nor love thy Life, nor hate; but what thou liv'st
> Live well, how long or short permit to Heaven..."

Adam sees the beginning of music, the beginning of metal work. He sees just men turned aside by rich and fair women into a life of ease, pleasure, and happiness. Adam at first thinks this is fine. He thanks the angel for this vision which seems better than the one of murder or the one of illness. This one seems to indicate nature's fulfillment.

But Michael answers, 603 ff., that he should not judge best by pleasure. Those tents of pleasure are the tents of wickedness, the homes of the descendants of Cain who killed his brother. They have beautiful women, but they have no spiritual allegiance and are empty of all good. They will corrupt the Sons of God, and soon the whole world will weep for them. He mentions the flood.

Adam answers, 632 ff., that it is a shame, but he sees that man's trouble is still the same: Women!

The angel says, 634 ff., it's man's "effeminate slackness" that started it. Man was made with better sense.

Now they see war, giants fighting, fields full of corpses and blood, cities besieged. One of those among the warring people speaks of God and justice, and the wicked ones are ready to kill him, but a cloud comes and snatches him away. Violence continues with refuge for none. Adam cries, asking the angel, 675 ff., about the men who multiply the sin of Cain by ten thousand and the one who is saved by Heaven.

Michael answers, 683 ff., that these wicked giants are the product of those ill-mated marriages Adam say between the Sons of God and the daughters of Cain. They thought a hero was one who killed and conquered, getting fame by what ought most to be abhorred. The one who was saved was Enoch, seventh from Adam. His case will show Adam the reward for righteousness. If Adam will watch, he'll see the reward for wickedness.

War ends. Everyone dives into pleasure, feasting, dancing. Among them comes a prophet to turn them back to God, but they pay no heed. The prophet, Noah, finally builds an ark wherein his family and some of each kind of living thing may be enclosed. The rain comes and all that is left of mankind and living birds and animals floats in one small boat.

Here, 754 ff., Milton addresses Adam and says how Adam cried another flood of tears, until the angel lifted him up, a father mourning the destruction of all his children.

Adam says, 763 ff., that he wishes he had never known the future, 770 ff.,

> "..... Let no man seek
> Henceforth to be foretold what shall befall
> Him or his children, evil he may be sure,
> Which neither his foreknowing can prevent."

Adam thinks this is the end of man, for those in the ark will die of famine or anguish. He had hoped for better, but he sees "Peace to corrupt no less than war to waste."

Michael answers, 787 ff., that those who were bent on pleasure were those who first loved exploits, but had no true virtue. They had killed and conquered for fame, title and riches. They had then turned to pleasure and corrupted even the peace. And, 797 ff.,

> "The conquered also, and enslaved by War
> Shall with their freedom lost all virtue lose
> And fear of God....."

Because they had pretended to be pious, their false religion had not protected them in battle. They have lost faith, and now are trying to live secure on what their conquerors will let them. And there is enough on earth that they may gorge themselves; so temperance may be tried. And then comes Noah, who alone, is instructed to build the ark. The angel explains the scenes of the flood. He says that Paradise will be pushed out with all its verdure ruined, and made into a salt island. For God gives no sanctity to a place unless men bring it with them.

Adam now sees the ark light on the mountain; the waters dry up. The dove goes out and returns with a leaf. The rainbow appears and Adam says, 870 ff., that his hope is renewed, now that man shall live and all the creatures. The sorrow of a wicked world of sons lost, finds compensation in one man, perfect and just. He asks about the rainbow, "distended as the Brow of God appeased" or does it bind the fluid skirts of the cloud to keep the rain from coming again.

Michael says, 884 ff., that Adam has the right idea, that one man's faithfulness made God relent, and the rainbow is a promise not to destroy the earth again by flood, but to let it go on until fire makes all things new, and a new Heaven and a new Earth appear.

Commentary
Action starts with Adam and Eve praying. Their prayers heard, Michael comes to reveal to Adam the future, and to drive the pair from Paradise.

Certain questions arise out of the argument. When the Son intercedes for man and tells how sweet repentant prayers are, is Milton saying that to rise above evil is better than complete innocence? This struggle to rise accounts for the very human arts: music, poetry, painting.

If God could soften the heart of man, couldn't he have softened the heart of Satan? There were times when Satan was close to repentance.

The reader should notice how the attitude of both Adam and

Eve changes after prayer. Adam's new faith and peace make him more tender and understanding with Eve; and Eve, instead of blaming everyone else, takes all the blame herself.

Milton had experience with human relations in politics, in the church and in his own tempestuous emotional life. He knew something about women, as evidenced in Eve's mourning about leaving home. This has been women's complaint since man first started west. The reader should remember that Milton wrote three hundred years ago opinions that still hold true today.

For example, his description of a hero as one who killed and conquered, getting fame by what should be most abhorred, fits today as well as Milton's time. The disintegrating effect of a total pursuit of pleasure, and the hypocrisy of the church—those who pretend to be pious but are really empty—and the loss of liberty with attendant loss of integrity—all remind us of present day conditions where people prefer security at any cost. Milton's words, 836 ff., are still true.

> ".... that God attributes to place
> No sanctity, if none be thither brought
> By men who there frequent, or therein dwell."

Milton's description of the ways men die, came from experience. He lived through the great plague of London, civil war in England, church conflict between Puritan and Cavalier. He had been imprisoned for his beliefs. When he talked about trouble, he knew his material. When he described a pest house, he told what he had seen. When he told about old age, he was thinking of his blindness and the handicaps of his own physical decline.

Of all the sins, Milton most deplored intemperance. His was the Greek idea of "not too much." He names intemperance as Eve's sin, the sin of Adam's children. Although capable of intense devotion and loyalty, Milton tried not to go to extremes. A nominal Puritan, he loved music (not accepted by Puritans) and enjoyed the wide field of the classics rather than the more narrow interest of the Puritans.

BOOK TWELVE

Summary
    The angel pauses between the destruction of the pre-flood world and the beginning of the new to see if Adam has any comment. When Adam says nothing, Michael says, 6 ff., that it is too hard on Adam to witness actual events. From now on the angel will relate what is to be.

For a while after the flood, men remain true to God and live in peace, but finally an ambitious one wants to rule his brothers. Nimrod, the mighty hunter and his followers find the mouth of Hell and out of the stuff therein build brick for a city and a tower that will reach Heaven, just in case God tries to destroy man again. God sees what they are doing, changes their languages; they can not continue their work and fall into quarreling while Heaven laughs. The tower is named Confusion or Babel.

Then Adam, like a father, says, 69-70, "man over men He made not Lord." That wretched man should not have put up his tower in defiance of God. How could he hope to breathe if not to starve?

The angel continues, 79 ff., that Adam rightly condemns that son who tried to take liberty from his brothers, but since the fall all true liberty is lost. Liberty always twins with Reason. Reason in man is obscured; then he falls prey to inordinate desires and upstart passions which rule him, and he is no longer free, 90 ff.,

> "......since he permits
> Within himself unworthy Powers to reign
> Over free Reason, God in Judgment just
> Subjects him from without to violent Lords."

Nevertheless the violent lords have no excuse for tyranny. But sometimes nations fall so low that their downfall is just. First they lose the inward liberty, then the outward. For example, he mentions Ham, the son of Noah who shamed his father, and was cursed as being Servant of Servants. Just so, many will lose their inward light until God chooses one nation and selects Abraham to raise up a people to serve God. Abraham, from Ur of Chaldea, receives the promise, 147 ff.,

> ".........that all Nations of the Earth
> Shall in his Seed be blessed; by that Seed
> Is meant thy great deliverer, who shall bruise
> The Serpent's head....."

The angel tells of Jacob's journey into Egypt, of his death, of the enslavement of the children of Jacob, and of their delivery by Moses and Aaron. He names the plagues and tells how the king finally lets the children of Israel go, 190 ff.,

> ".....Thus with ten wounds
> The River-dragon tamed at length submits
> To let his sojourners depart."

The story continues with the crossing of the Red Sea, how the chosen people are protected from the pursuing Pharoah, of how the cloud covers them by day and the fire by night, how they go through the desert, not straight to Canaan because terror of war might turn them back to Egypt, preferring slavery to hardship.

Also by their delay in the wilderness, they can set up their government in accordance with the laws given by God from Mount Sinai and with sacrifices ordained to remind them of the prophecy that the seed of Abraham will bruise the Serpent and effect man's deliverance.

The people are afraid of God's voice so Moses serves as Mediator, forerunner of the Messiah. Then God is pleased with men and sets up his tabernacle with them so that He may dwell with them. Finally they come to the promised land where there is much to tell of battles and victories.

Adam interrupts, 270 ff., thanking the angel for his information but wondering why man has so many laws, which must mean they have many sins. If this be so, how can God live with them?

Michael answers, 285 ff., that man will live under sin, and that the laws are given to show up their sins. They will see that they are sinful, but can't remove the guilt even by the blood of bulls and goats. This way they will know that a better sacrifice must be offered. In time they will learn the better covenant, 303 ff.,

"From shadowy Types to Truth, from Flesh to Spirit,
    From imposition of strict Laws, to free
    Acceptance of large Grace, from servile fear
    To filial, works of Law to works of Faith."

And therefore Moses, being the minister of law, may not lead his people into Canaan, but Joshua, symbol of Jesus will lead them, even as Jesus will lead, 313 ff.,

"....... long-wandered Man
    Safe to eternal Paradise of rest."

Meanwhile the children of Abraham shall dwell and prosper in Canaan, but when they sin, God raises enemies. When they repent, he saves them. Of the royal stock will come David, and he will be ancestor of the Messiah who will reign forever. David's son, Solomon, will build a temple; then the chosen people, sinful again, will be carried away into Babylon for seventy years. Upon their return, they will first rebuild the house of God, and for a while have peace, but again they quarrel and the priests, who should have been most righteous, seize power, then lose it to a stranger, so that the true Messiah will be born barred of his right. Michael tells of the star proclaiming Christ's birth, the eastern sages and the angels singing to the shepherds.

When Adam hears that at last the Messiah has been born, he cries for joy. Now he understands, 375 ff., what the prophecy means that the Seed of Woman should bruise the Serpent.

Michael answers, 386 ff., that Adam must not think of the fight between the Son and Satan as a duel, or as being concerned with literal wounds, but that the Son defeats Satan by destroying the power of Satan over mankind. To fulfill for Adam's lack of obedience, the Son shall live hated, persecuted, and crucified, but with him crucified are both the laws that condemn and the sins of man.

So the Son dies, but lives again to offer life to man, 427 ff.,

> "....This God-like act
> Annuls thy doom, the death thou shouldst have died,
> In sin forever lost from life."

This blow defeats Satan, Sin and Death, a blow far worse than the temporal death the Son dies (the bruising of the Victor's heel) or the temporal death that God's people die which is, 434 ff.,

> ".......a death like sleep,
> A gentle wafting to immortal Life."

After resurrection the Son will not stay long on earth, but will leave his mission to men who will teach all nations. The Son returns to Heaven in victory with the Serpent chained. The Son stays with God until the end of the World when he will judge. The faithful will have the New Earth, all Paradise, a happier place than Eden ever was.

Adam praises God's goodness, 469 ff., that he can make such good out of evil, a feat more wonderful than when he first made light out of darkness. Adam doesn't know whether to repent or to rejoice. Then he wonders what will happen to the faithful whom the Son leaves on earth.

The angel answers, 485 ff., that of course, the faithful will suffer, but they will have a Comforter, who will guide them, help them resist evil, and die unafraid. They will win many to their way, but at last they will die and in their place will come wolves for teachers who will pervert the mysteries of Heaven to their own vile advantage and tradition. They will want names, places, and titles, and will join secular powers, though pretending to act in a spiritual way. They will enforce spiritual laws by carnal power—laws never written by God and not given by God who gives to each man alike. Persecution will come on all those who persist in true worship; but the greater part will, 534 ff.,

> "...deem in outward Rites and specious forms
>   Religion satisfied.....
>   ....So shall the World go on,
>   To good malignant, to bad men benign..."

Then the Saviour will return in the clouds of Heaven, raise the world from its flames, destroy Satan and evil and found a New Heaven and a New Earth for eternal happiness.

Then Adam remarks, 553 ff., on how fast the angel has told the whole story of earth, beyond which is eternity. Adam has found peace in the knowledge, which is all his mind can hold, 561 ff.,

> ".....that to obey is best,
>   And love with fear the only God..."

He determines to worship God, and by good overcome evil and by small things accomplish great, and remain faithful until death which is the gate of life, a truth he knows from the story of the Redeemer.

Michael answers, 575 ff., that Adam has learned the sum of wisdom, and that if he knew every secret of the universe, it would be of no more value than what he now knows. He advises, 581 ff.,

> ".......only add
>   Deeds to thy knowledge answerable, add Faith,
>   Add Virtue, Patience, Temperance, add Love,
>   By name to come called Charity, the soul
>   Of all the rest: then wilt thou not be loth
>   To leave this Paradise, but shalt possess
>   A Paradise within thee, happier far."

They must now descend for the hour of their exit from Paradise approaches. Adam wakens Eve, for in her dreams she has learned submission and resignation. Adam will tell her what he has learned, particularly that her seed will save mankind. Then both in one faith, they will live long though sad, to meditate the happy ending.

Eve says, 610 ff., that God has given in her sleep great hint of good. She is ready to go wherever Adam leads, 615 ff.,

> "In me is no delay; with thee to go,
> Is to stay here; without thee here to stay,
> Is to go hence unwilling; thou to me
> Art all things under Heaven, all places thou
> Who for my wilful crime are banished hence."

Eve carries with her the promised Seed that will restore all. Adam, pleased with her speech, doesn't answer because the Archangel stands too near, and the other angels come in a flame. Michael takes "our lingering parents" in either hand and guides them down into the plain. When they look back they see the guardian flame over the gate to Paradise, and, 646 ff.,

> "The world was all before them, where to choose
> Their place of rest, and Providence their guide.
> They hand in hand with wandering steps and slow,
> Through Eden took their solitary way."

Commentary

Action concerns what takes place after the flood, until the end of the World. In order to shorten his story, Milton has Michael narrate instead of showing scenes. This affords a change of pace to help hold the reader's attention.

Again in Milton's description of how the church falls away from its first purity, he describes what he feels about the church in England, about the civil war, the rights of man, and man's desire for security rather than liberty. Have conditions changed in three hundred years?

He repeats the theme that man may rise from flesh to spirit, from law to freedom. He had propounded this even before the fall of man, V, 497 ff., and VII, 157 ff. He says that Paradise is within, just as he said Hell was within.

Milton describes the New Earth as a happier place than Eden ever was. This repeats the idea of XI, 26 ff., that the prayers of the repentant sinners are sweeter than the flowers of Paradise. Milton seems to be saying that it would be better to remain innocent, but with free choice, a man is bound to fall, and he can attain a higher place than if he had never had free choice, had never fallen.

Milton states his belief that each man's conscience ought to guide him in religious experience, 488 ff.,

> "...upon their hearts shall write,
> To guide them in all truth.....
> The Spirit of God, promised alike and given
> To all Believers.....or what the Spirit within
> Shall on the heart engrave.....
> ....built by Faith to stand,
> Their own Faith, not another's...."

This refutes any claim by any church to have final authority over man's conscience.

ANALYSIS AND DISCUSSION

PLOT

The plot with Miltonic embellishments follows the Biblical story of the fall of Satan, man's creation, his fall and the plan of redemption. The conflict lies between good and evil. God, the Son, and the good angels compete with Satan, Sin, Death, and the fallen angels for the soul of created Mankind. Satan vows to seduce and destroy man; Christ volunteers to save him.

Conflict between God and Satan arises when Satan (Lucifer) through pride, wants to be equal with God. After force fails to gain him victory, he resorts to fraud, seduces Man, but is sentenced to destruction by the Son who will take man's place in proving obedience and in bearing punishment.

As soon as man has fallen, conflict arises within man himself, between Adam and Eve. Nature turns unfriendly. When Adam sees what will happen to his descendants, he views man in every kind of distress, but always the struggle lies between good and evil.

Milton treats the Biblical account as literal truth, although the theology may now be considered outdated. He talks of Heaven, Hell, and other places in the universe as if they had material dimensions. There are gates to Heaven and a stairway, celestial animated chariots; even angels can eat and digest food.

The modern reader may consider the story as fable, parable, or allegory. He may find fault with the astronomy, the science, the theology, and certainly the logic. Can there be foreknowing without predestination? If God made all things did he not also make sin? Milton says that free will admits the possibility of choice, and therefore of sin.

Certain action will appear foolish to the reader. Why guard the gates of Hell while Man was being created when everyone knew what would happen? Why send Raphael to warn Adam when the outcome was already certain? The fact is that admitted free choice necessitates two possibilities, one of which is better than the other. Milton's attempt to square this with God's foreknowledge and his omnipotence makes for difficult reasoning at times.

The poem therefore, is a vehicle to discuss Milton's theory of how to justify God's way to man, as stated in the opening lines, and also to resolve Milton's own doubts.

The broad action is simple, the ramifications infinite. There is a great deal of narrative of both past and future. Sometimes there is drama itself. Considering the book covers the whole history of the World, there is little action on the stage. We hear half of the book through the voices of Raphael, Michael, and Adam. Sometimes

Milton interrupts with a prayer, a comment to God or to Adam or to the reader. Sometimes in the middle of an epic speech the orator will speak in an aside to Adam or to someone else, or Milton will put in an aside, himself.

Sometimes the speeches slow up the action, often Milton's allusions slow up action. But the speeches are a vehicle on which to hang the events, and the allusions give the rich depth to the poem.

SETTING

The setting of *Paradise Lost* comprises Heaven, Hell, Paradise, and Earth. Since no one can state anything about the reality of those first three, the settings must be judged on their artistic and symbolic merit. Milton says that he (and his characters) will attempt to explain Heavenly things by earthly.

He makes the reader see the "darkness visible" of Hell, the fallen angels grasping false fruit that looks like that of the Tree of Knowledge of Good and Evil, and having it turn to bitter ashes. Hell is a place of flames, of despair and ever-burning sulphur. The fiends dig up gold and precious metals and build Pandemonium. Victims in Hell are alternately frozen then burned. However, Milton makes it clear that Hell is a state of mind.

It is more difficult for the reader to visualize Heaven, with its "ambrosial fragrance," its heavenly choirs, its angels with crowns of gold and flowers that never fade. When the angels throw off their garlands, the jasper sea is "impurpled with celestial roses."

Heaven, just before Lucifer rebelled, looked like this, V, 627 ff.,

"..........Evening now approached
(For we have also our Evening and our Morn,
We ours for change delectable, not need)
Forthwith from dance to sweet repast they turn
Desirous; all in Circles as they stood,
Tables are set, and on a sudden piled
With Angels' Food, and rubied Nectar flows

> In Pearl, in Diamond, and massy Gold,
> Fruit of delicious Vines, the growth of Heaven.
> On flowers reposed, and with fresh flowerets crowned,
> They eat, they drink, and in communion sweet
> Quaff immortality and joy....."

Stars and heavenly bodies move in a sacred dance, V, 177 ff. Perhaps other stars dance round the Sun, VIII, 122 ff., Satan in his lament IX, 103 thinks,

> "Terrestrial Heaven, danced round by other Heavens
> That shine,...."

Heaven is a place of harmony, music, beauty, happiness.

Paradise, before the fall of Man, is much like Heaven, as Satan has just observed, quote above. A profusion of plants and flowers, fruit trees, friendly animals and birds, golden fishes live in a climate that is always peaceful spring. The harmony of Paradise symbolizes innocence.

After the fall of man, the Earth changes. Adam and Eve quarrel. Nature turns unfriendly. In Adam's preview of what will happen, he sees the earth corrupted to the place where God sends the flood, the culmination of outraged Nature's revulsion against Sin. The change in Nature symbolizes separation from God through loss of innocence.

With such a broad setting as the then known universe, background must be broad and generalized, almost altogether symbolic.

CHARACTERS

Satan, One of the best realized characters and considered by some critics to be the hero of *Paradise Lost,* appears as a magnificent, sympathetic personality, who chooses evil and degenerates to a bestial level. The reader can understand the struggle within Satan, better than he can understand abstract goodness. Satan has a keen mind, a way of inspiring loyalty. He never gives up, knows how to win others to his way of thinking and to get them to act.

For example, when he talks to the fallen angels on the lake of fire, he taunts them by asking if they are waiting for God to send thunderbolts to pin them to the bottom of the lake. When he talks to Sin and Death, he makes them believe his trip to Earth is for their sole benefit. He does the same with Chaos, convincing him that if Satan wins, Chaos will get the World back in his domain.

Although Satan knows he is making his own Hell, he sticks to his plan; his pride will not permit him to submit.

In Book I, of the three descriptions of Satan, the first emphasizes his size and the horror of his fall. The second shows his leadership and the third his lost divinity. He weeps, feels responsible for the fallen angels. Three times he tries to talk; three times he chokes up.

Satan's likable aspect is shown when he advises the angels to amuse themselves in Hell while he goes to Earth. Sometimes he admits to himself his pride, that his punishment is just, that Hell lies within him; but he chooses to forsake hope, fear, and remorse. He makes this same evil choice every time — each time he sees some new beauty, he is recalled to the sense of his loss, as when he sees Man whom he could so easily love because he is like God.

Whenever the reader sees Satan in the clutch of what is left of his conscience, the reader knows how Satan will choose and the knowledge makes the passage more poignant.

Satan's leadership is illustrated by how he manipulates his angels so that none will offer to go to Earth with him. Though the offer would be turned down, the one offering would gain prestige which Satan does not want to allow a subordinate. His arrogant self-confidence comes to his defense when, as a toad tempting Eve, he feels the touch of the angel's scepter and turns back automatically into himself. The angels don't recognize him, and he scorns their rank saying they can't be very important because all the higher ranks know him. They retort with a reminder of how his luster is impaired; he does not shine as formerly.

In his altercation with Gabriel, he says first that he came to Earth to better his plight. When Gabriel questions his leadership by asking if the others like Hell and wish to stay there, Satan changes his argument saying he came to spy out the land. He adds that they can't prove a thing against him, and calls Gabriel a "proud limitary Cherub."

When Satan rebels against Heaven, he acts like a natural troublemaker. He appeals to the pride of his followers, says their duty will be doubled, urges them to cast off their yoke for they are as good as anybody. He sounds like a typical rabble rouser, V, 772 ff.

The reader will note a gradual degeneration in Satan's responses. In Book IV, 32 ff., he is full of sorrow, but in Book IX, 99 ff., he is bitter and despairing. In Book VI, 156 ff., he says Abdiel has opposed one third part of the gods. In Book IX, 141, he claims to have liberated almost one half of the angels.

Whereas earlier Satan has admitted to himself God's justice, he begins to attribute to God his own evil motives. He accuses God of making man out of spite. But Satan is not so far down but that he shudders at the idea of incarnating himself in the bestial slime of the snake.

Having chosen Evil, Satan uses every guile to tempt Eve. He flatters her, asks her what is one man's admiration when she should be a goddess with gods to worship her. He pretends indignation at the deprivation suffered by not eating of the Tree of Knowledge. He calls her a goddess and begs her to eat. All the brilliance of his mind has turned to Evil. In the end, of course, he is chained by the Son and sealed up forever in Hell.

Beelzebub, next to Satan in rank, echoes Satan's ideas. He lets others talk until he gets the drift of opinion, then offers Satan's idea of getting revenge through man. He is Satan's right-hand man.

Mammon loves gold, builds a jeweled and golden palace. He doesn't want war, thinks they can imitate Heaven with gold and jewels. Mammon is pure materialist.

Moloch, a man of action, wants war and destruction. He is the blood-thirsty warrior, who will want sacrifices of little children.

Belial, false double-dealer votes for sloth. When Satan opens his guns on the good angels, Belial jokes about the weight of terms they are sending and the lack of understanding (poor footing) of the good angels who roll in their armor.

The rest of the evil angels and false gods do not achieve personality and serve as types of false beliefs and worships of different times and places.

Sin, half woman and half snake, obeys Satan, has a secret unity with him, builds a road to connect Hell with Earth.

Death, a ravenous, carniverous corpse tells of his hunger, how he smells decay on Earth. He achieves a loathesome personality when he wanders through the pest houses withholding his dart, though men plead for it.

Of the forces of Good, the *Son* is most nearly realized, more so when he becomes also the Son of Man. For the most part He is Power for Good, but becomes human in his desire to clothe Adam and Eve against the change in weather. He represents God and sometimes the remarks about them indicate that Milton thinks of them as one person.

God (sometimes including Christ) shows a sense of humor by leaving some things unknown so he can laugh at man's explanations for them. He teases Adam when he wants a mate, but eventually gives Adam what he wants. Both Son and Father seem abstractions of Good.

Of the good angels, *Abdiel* (who probably stands for Milton himself) stands alone against one-third of Heaven. *Uriel* guards the sun, *Raphael*, companionable, blushes when Adam asks about love among the angels. *Michael*, more severe, is a fighter. His restrained attitude toward man, may be accounted for by the fact that Raphael visits Adam before the fall, Michael after.

Gabriel is a good top sergeant.

Adam first appears noble, tall, God-like erect, and innocent, but curious — wondering why the Tree of Knowledge is forbidden. He tries to understand everything, rationalizes Eve's dream of the Tree. He is cautious about too much knowledge, careful not to ask too much. He shows determination and spirit in arguing with God about a proper mate.

Adam tells Raphael how wonderful Eve and marriage are, but when Raphael reproves him for too much admiration of Eve's physical beauty, Adam says it isn't really sex, but all the little charming things she does. He is admitting how he feels, not how he acts. Of course, soon enough, he will act just as he has thought.

After the angel's reproof Adam turns the tables by asking Raphael about love among the angels, and is rewarded by an angel's blush.

Although Adam doesn't lack courage, he can't handle Eve. Not brutal enough to force her to stay, he tries to talk her into staying and finally says if he keeps her against her will, it is better for her to go.

When Adam sins, he does so deliberately because of his passion for Eve. He is not deceived. But after the fall, he complains about the "false worm" to whom she listened and says she would have to be seen though by the Devil himself.

He is most human in his lament and self-searching when he wishes to die, but wonders if death would really be the end. He worries about his children, argues to himself the justice of God. He does not respond to Eve's first attempt at reconciliation, but finally relents and comforts her, gives her advice from his superior wisdom.

In viewing what will happen to his offspring, Adam is a spectator but comes to life once in a while when he cries and when he says that he sees now that it is true as always that women are the cause of all trouble in the world.

Eve, the best realized character after Satan, exhibits natural vanity which makes her prefer her own image to that of Adam. But she turns to Adam, her natural master, for comfort when she has had a bad dream. She is warm-hearted, good-natured, a careful housekeeper. But she is willful, determined to work apart from Adam and prove herself. When he does not give permission, she assumes it and goes.

At her temptation she rationalizes her sin; and after eating the fruit, she determines one way or another to take Adam with her. Unlike Adam, Eve is not afraid of knowledge, nor does she hesitate to call God, the Great Forbidder.

When she brings the fruit to Adam, she claims falsely that she wanted the godhead for Adam. She is delighted when Adam prefers her to God. When Adam blames her for the fall, she says it is his fault. He knew she was weak and he should have made her stay with him. He practically forced her into sin. If she couldn't leave Adam's side, she'd better have stayed a rib.

With more impulsive courage than Adam she suggests they kill themselves. But typically feminine, she prefaces her remark by saying she knows he won't listen to her. Eve is emotional, not intellectual. It is she who offers first to make up with Adam after their quarrel. She admits her fault and takes the blame.

Woman-like Eve hates to leave her home, but is at last reconciled to go wherever Adam goes — hand in hand through Eden, comforted that she carries within her their first child.

IDEA

Milton wrote *Paradise Lost* to expound certain ideas, the main one being to justify God's ways to Man. This is the epic idea, with action inherent in the universal nature of the subject.

Certain themes appear over and over in the poem. Danger lies in man himself, IX, 348 ff. A mind is its own Hell, I, 254 ff. Satan carries Hell within him, IV, 20 ff. A mind is its own Paradise, XII, 586 ff. All of these add up to an exposition of the power of the mind.

Next to the power of mind comes man's free will and human responsibility. Raphael says, V, 532, that hearts not free can't be tried. God says, III, 98 ff., when he sees Satan heading for Paradise, and knows man will fall,

"..... I made him just and right,
Sufficient to have stood, though free to fall."
.....

"Not free, what proof could they have given sincere...
Where only what they needs must do, appeared,
Not what they would?"

Coupled with free will is the dignity of man. Raphael, V, 372 ff., says man was created and given a place where Heavenly spirits might visit. Again, VIII, 218 ff., Raphael says:

"....... for God on thee
Abundantly his gifts hath also poured
....
Nor less think we in Heaven of thee on Earth
Than of our fellow-servant..."

The dignity of man is proven by God's willingness to sacrifice his Son for man, III, 274 ff., and the Son becomes eternally the Son of God and man, III, 316.

Moloch says the proper motion of spirits is upward, II, 75 ff. Adam says he wanted to go upward, VIII, 259 ff., when he first awakened, newly-made. Mankind may be led from light to light upward, III, 195 ff., and he is led from flesh to spirit, V, 404 ff., and 469 ff. Satan said, II, 432-3 "Long is the way and hard, that out of

Hell leads up to light." But the struggle avails something, for re-deemed man is more valuable than untried innocence.

Conversely Satan chooses Evil and physical degradation fol-lows. He loses luster, his brightness dimmed. Finally he is a snake. Likewise Adam, IX, 887, sees distemper in Eve's cheek, and both Adam and Eve reveal in their faces their spiritual loss, X, 11 ff.

The great sins are pride and intemperance, whereas the great virtue is temperance — the Greek idea of not too much, XI, 530 ff. Before the fall man ate enough but not too much, V, 451-2. Giving themselves to ungoverned appetite meant forsaking God's image, XI, 515 ff. One should be temperate even in knowledge, VII, 111 ff.

Nothing may happen but God wills it. Beelzebub says that God will have his way, II, 323 ff., and Gabriel tells Satan, IV, 1006 ff., that they are doing only as much as God permits. God's control over what happens seems to contradict man's free will. Milton tries to reconcile the two.

God is everywhere, XI, 335 ff., and no place has sanctity un-less man's attitude brings it, XI, 836 ff.

Fallen spirits retain some of their divinity, II, 482 ff. It is this quality that makes Satan so fascinating.

Milton thinks woman inferior to man, IV, 440 ff., and Adam is Eve's law, IV, 635 ff. Woman is subject to man, VIII, 561 ff. Mil-ton thinks in such an arrangement lies true happiness.

STYLE AND TECHNIQUE

Milton's characteristics are: (1) a Puritan interest in God's dealings with man, (2) a Renaissance love for the beauty of lan-guage, music of poetry, music itself, and (3) a scholar's interest in Classical, Biblical, historical, and scientific learning.

He states at the beginning of *Paradise Lost* that the poem will be written in English heroic verse without rime, as Homer in Greek and Virgil in Latin. He will use earthly examples to explain other not-earthly places.

VIEWPOINT

At various places in the poem, Milton prays for inspiration, and he believes that his story comes from a higher source. The story is told from various viewpoints, there being long speeches by Satan and his cohorts and by God, the Son, and various angels. Adam tells his story; Eve talks also. Milton interposes with prayers, exhortations, laments, and asides. About half the story is narrative; the other half is drama and prolonged dialogue. Raphael and Michael are the chief angel narrators.

SYMBOLISM

The whole story is symbolic, so that it would be impossible to point out each example. Milton makes light stand for good, darkness for evil. Because of his blindness, light has a special significance for him.

Satan, flying with fire rolling off him, I, 222 ff., is a symbol of darkness and passion. The serpent with its red eye also symbolizes passion. Satan, his glory obscured from sin is like, I, 594 ff.,

.... "the sun new risen
Looks through the Horizontal misty Air
Shorn of his Beams......"

In sinning, he has lost his light or goodness. And he addresses the Sun (symbol of Good) with hate, IV, 32 ff.

Adam prays God to dispel evil as day dispels night, V, 206 ff.

Of itself the sun is barren, meaning that abstract good has no value. But the sun comes to fruition on earth, III, 609 ff.; so good comes to fruition here.

The change of weather after the fall symbolized death. The

harmony of Paradise symbolized innocence; the confusion, sin.

IMAGERY & ALLUSION

It would be impossible to discuss imagery without allusion, since the richest parts of the poem are built of these. For example, the odors of Eden are like those of spices wafted to sailors who go around the Cape of Hope. The activities of fallen angels are patterned after the Olympian games held in honor of Zeus, or the Pythian held in honor of Apollo.

Milton's invocation to the Heavenly muse, I, 1 ff., reflects mythological and classical background. He mentions Orion, I, 305 ff., whom Virgil connects with rains and storm as causing the Red Sea to overthrow Busiris (representing Pharaoh) when Israel fled. Here in a few lines he touches mythology, Biblical history, and history.

Milton says the odor of Paradise is better to Satan than the odor of burning fish was to Asmodeus. This refers to a legend of Tobit's son, IV, 166 ff., who married a girl beloved of an evil spirit, Asmodeus. To chase out the spirit, Tobit burns the heart and liver of a fish, which smells so bad the evil spirit is driven into Egypt where an angel binds him.

Satan is like a prowling wolf, IV, 183 ff., entering the sheepfold, or a thief climbing in through a window, or like one of the "lewd hirelings" of the church.

Another description of Satan, I, 284 ff., says his shield hangs on his back like the moon, and compared to his spear, the tallest Norwegian pine would be but a wand. He calls to his troops, 302 ff., scattered like leaves on the lake of fire, I, 315, and all Hell resounds. The fallen angels hear and rise like the locusts in the plague of Egypt and fill all the plain, more than the barbarians who will invade the Roman Empire.

Pharaoh becomes the river dragon with ten wounds, XII, 190 ff.

Personification abounds in *Paradise Lost*. Prayers are alive, XI, 14 ff.

> "...........To Heaven their prayers
> Flew up, nor missed the way, by envious winds
> Blown vagabond or frustrate: in they passed
> Dimensionless through Heavenly doors; then clad
> With incense, where the Golden Altar fumed
> By their great Intercessor, came in sight
> Before the Father's throne."

In the description of the drying of the flood, XI, 841 ff., the clouds flee, the face of the flood is wrinkled as in old age, the sun gazes and drinks, the water steals with soft foot toward the Ocean which has stopped its overflowing while Heaven has shut her gates.

> "........for the clouds were fled,
> Driven by a keen North-wind, that blowing dry
> Wrinkled the face of Deluge, as decayed;
> And the clear Sun on his wide Watery Glass
> Gazed hot, and of the fresh wave largely drew,
> As after thirst, which made their flowing shrink
> From standing lake to tripping ebb, that stole
> With soft foot towards the Deep, who now had stopped
> His Sluices, as the Heaven his windows shut."

In the following quotation appeals are made to the eye, ear, and sense of touch. Silence, Evening, Twilight, and the Moon are personified. IV, 598 ff.,

> "Now came still Evening on, and Twilight gray
> Had in her sober Livery all things clad;
> Silence accompanied, for Beast and Bird,
> They to their grassy Couch, these to their Nests
> Were slunk, all but the wakeful Nightingale;
> She all night long her amorous descant sung;
> Silence was pleased. Now glowed the Firmament
> With living Sapphires; Hesperus that led
> The starry Host, rode brightest, till the Moon

Riding in clouded Majesty, at length
Apparent Queen unveiled her peerless light
And o'er the dark her Silver Mantle threw."

Milton describes, IV, 248, "Groves whose rich trees wept odorous gums and balm," and IV, 34-5, "all the stars hide their diminished heads."

Typical references to music are the similes used in the description of the building of the capitol of Hell. Filling a mold was like, I, 708 ff.,

"As in an Organ from one blast of wind
To many a row of Pipes the sound-bored breathes."

and the capitol of Hell, I, 711 ff.,

"Rose like an Exhalation, with the sound
of Dulcet Symphonies and voices sweet..."

Other references showing the power of music are, II, 552 ff.,

"Their song was partial, but the harmony.....
Suspended Hell..."

and, I, 551 ff., he speaks of music

".......such as raised
To highth of noblest temper Heroes old
Arming to Battle, and instead of rage
Deliberate valor breathed...."

Of the many references to sunrises and sunsets and light, one example will suffice here, IV, 540 ff.,

".........the setting Sun
Slowly descended, and with right aspect
Against the eastern Gate of Paradise
Leveled his evening Rays."

In discussing Milton's allusions, the reader should note that he refers to current happenings in England, for example his description of pest houses, the emptiness of church forms, civil conflict, and loss of liberty. He speaks of Galileo whom he had met in Italy, I, 287 ff.,

> "....the moon, whose Orb
> Through Optic Glass the Tuscan artist views
> At evening from the top of Fesole,
> Or in Valdarno..."

Coming also under imagery would be Milton's use of contrast to impress his reader. In describing Hell, he compares the evil angels, I, 768 ff., to bees in springtime when they go out among the fresh dews and flowers. This mention of spring and dew and flowers makes Hell more terrible. In Hell victims go from burning to freezing. However, his use of contrast comes often in word usage.

WORD USAGE

In III, 380, Milton describes God's brightness as "dark with excessive bright." Also in II, 623-4,

> "Created evil, for evil only good,
> Where all life dies, death lives..."

Instead of actual contrast, sometimes he uses repetition of one word with shaded meanings, as Eve's speech when she leaves Paradise, XII, 615 ff.,

> "....with thee to go,
> Is to stay here, without thee here to stay,
> Is to go hence unwilling..."

or, V, 235 ff.,

> "Happiness in his power left free to will,
> Left to his own free Will, his will though free
> Yet mutable."

Another favorite Miltonian use of words is to employ an adjective for a noun, for example, II, 278, "the sensible of pain," or II, 406, "the palpable obscure," or II, 409, "the vast abrupt."

Inverted word order would come naturally to a Latin scholar, for example, IV, 850, "luster visibly impaired," and IV, 856, "against thee wicked and thence weak," and IV, 870, "faded splendor wan."

An example of alliteration is, V, 578,

> "Reigned where these Heavens now roll, where
>   Earth now rests
> Upon her Center poised, when on a day
> (For time, though in Eternity, applied
> To motion, measures all things durable."

First note repetition of r's, then of t's, then m's. Reading aloud of a passage from almost anywhere in the poem will show alliteration.

The use of onomatopoeia as well as alliteration may be illustrated by, XI, 743-4, "down rushed the rain impetuous..." and one can hear the hiss in X, 506 ff.,

> "..........he hears
> On all sides from innumerable tongues
> A dismal universal hiss, the sound
> Of public scorn..."

or in, IX, 164 ff.,

> "....am now constrained
> Into a Beast, and, mixed with bestial slime,
> This essence to incarnate..."

Alliteration may be combined with short words for power or monotony, as IX, 11, "That brought into this World a world of woe." Or IX, 48 ff.,

"The Sun was sunk, and after him the Star
of Hesperus..."

SATIRE

Milton's humor mostly turns to satire. He makes fun of
the Presbyterians, as well as the Church of England. He says in
an aside regarding the pleasure-seeking race before the flood, XI,
626, "erelong to swim at large." Adam says Eve would have to be
seen though by the Devil himself. Belial ridicules the good angels
who roll in their armor when the guns are fired at them. God laughs
at man's attempts to explain the universe.

SENTENCE STRUCTURE

Sentences are long, involved, and sometimes inverted in word
order. The first sixteen lines of the poem are one sentence. If the
poem is read aloud, the sentence structure becomes less difficult
and alliteration adds to beauty and understanding of the work.

QUESTIONS

1. Why is Milton so concerned with Light? (VIII Commentary, III
   Summary, Symbolism)

2. What problem in logic does *Paradise Lost* present? (X Commentary, XI Commentary, Plot)

3. Show examples of Milton's understanding of human nature. (IX
   Summary and Commentary, X Summary and Commentary, XI
   Summary, Characters: Satan and Eve)

4. For what purpose did Milton write *Paradise Lost?* (Plot, Idea)

5. How does the character of Satan arouse the reader's sympathy?
   (I Commentary, IV Summary, Characters: Satan)

6. Give five ideas that Milton propounds in *Paradise Lost.* (Idea)

7. What is Milton's source of inspiration? (I Summary, VII Summary and Commentary, IX Summary, Viewpoint)

8. How does Milton use his life and experience in writing? (Introduction, III Commentary, XI Commentary)

9. Give examples of humor in this poem. (Characters, Satire)

10. What is the great conflict in *Paradise Lost?* In whom is it personified? (III Commentary, Plot)

11. What does Milton think of the place of women? (IV Summary, VIII Summary and Commentary, IX Commentary, X Summary and Commentary, Plot)

12. How do speakers in Hell reveal their characters? (II Summary and Characters)

13. Give examples of Milton's love of music. (II Commentary, Imagery) of sunrises. (V Commentary, VI Commentary, VII Commentary)

14. Point out three allusions: classical, Biblical, historical. (Imagery, II Commentary)

16. Find passages that illustrate alliterations. (Word Usage)

17. Show two places where Milton interrupts the story to speak as Milton, himself. (IV Summary, VIII Summary)

19 Point out three places where Milton emphasizes man's free will. (V Summary, VIII Summary, X Summary, Word Usage)

20. Give two examples of typical Milton word-usage. (II Commentary, III Commentary, VII Commentary, Word Usage)

21. Give two examples of personification. (I Commentary, Imagery)

22. In what way are Milton's remarks appropriate today? (IX Summary)

NOTES

NOTES

NOTES